How to Stop Smoking Through Self-Hypnosis

Leslie M. LeCron
California State Certified Psychologist

Introduction by MELVIN POWERS

Foreword by RAY LaSCOLA, M.D.

GULF COAST HYPNOSIS TRAINING CENTER
Miss Judy Foister, C.P.H., Director
Certified Medical Hypnotist
OFFICES IN
PANAMA CITY, FLORIDA
DOTHAN, ALABAMA
TALLAHASSEE, FLORIDA
FT. WALTON BEACH, FLORIDA
PENSACOLA, FLORIDA

Published by
Melvin Powers
WILSHIRE BOOK COMPANY
12015 Sherman Road
No. Hollywood, California 91605
Telephone: (213) 875-1711

Wilshire Book Company edition
is published by special arrangement
with Prentice-Hall, Inc., Englewood Cliffs, N. J.

L.C. Cat. Card No.: 64–21749

ISBN 0-87980-065-8

Printed by
HAL LEIGHTON PRINTING COMPANY
P.O. Box 3952
North Hollywood, California 91605
Telephone: (213) 983-1105

PRINTED IN THE UNITED STATES OF AMERICA

43497–B&P

INTRODUCTION

When Leslie M. LeCron wrote this book millions of
cigarette smokers were still hoping against hope that the
mounting evidence against the ubiquitous habit would
somehow prove false, and that a scapegoat could be found
to account for the alarming dangers which were becoming
associated statistically with an indulgence they wished to
continue thinking of as a harmless source of pleasure and
relaxation.

Fortunately for them, it is now clear, the tobacco industry
was unable to stem the tide of incontrovertible proof that
cigarettes were a definite hazard to health, and the legislation prophesied by Mr. LeCron in these pages was finally
enacted into law. A bill passed by Congress and the Senate
required tobacco companies to label every package of cigarettes manufactured after January 1, 1966 with the warning
that their product *could* be injurious to health. It was weaker
than the Surgeon General desired, but it was, at least, a mild
version of *caveat emptor* (let the buyer beware).

This labeling bill is a victory of sorts for public health
authorities, but experience indicates it will be of small value
unless smokers are made aware of a method that is uniformly
successful in ridding them of their pernicious habit—permanently and without the constant craving that in the past
has almost inevitably led to relapses in all but the most dedi-
cated and highly motivated individuals. Most medium-to-
heavy smokers will admit that they despair of ever breaking

the bonds of smoking, for the majority of them have struggled unsuccessfully with the problem in the past despite the fact they have outwardly maintained their indulgence was harmless, even beneficial.

It is these individuals that this book will help because Mr. LeCron's method has nothing to do with will power, a quality they admit they lacked sadly in previous confrontations in which they were faced down. But Mr. LeCron, one of the best known and respected hypnotherapists in the world, states that those who have constantly failed and feel hopelessly enslaved are precisely the ones he wishes to aid in breaking their shackles. Better still, he keeps his word. No one has ever failed who has followed his method fully.

This is a strong statement, but the writer knows Mr. LeCron and the techniques he utilizes and is happy to be able to corroborate the statement. Using his method which bypasses will power by substituting suggestion, hypnosis and/or self-hypnosis, stopping smoking becomes relatively easy. Pride of achievement and benefits to health more than compensate for the dubious satisfaction of smoking when the problem is approached in the proper manner.

There should no longer be any question about motivation. A habit that makes your chances of dying from lung cancer nine times as great as those of the non-smoker is the sort of habit you can devoutly desire to stop. Actually, as Mr. LeCron points out, there has probably never been any doubt about the motivation of most smokers. It is just that even downright terror of what may happen if they continue to practice their deadly habit has not been enough to offset wishful thinking and the smokescreens (no pun intended) laid down by those who have sought to obscure the issue.

However, documentation of the potentially lethal effects of smoking has now been proved beyond a shadow of doubt, and all the answers are still not in. The final answers are certain to be even more horrendous. At present, smoking at its worst produces lung cancer, and at its best a shortness of breath and general diminution of energy. In between it greatly increases one's chances of provoking heart attacks, emphysema, circulatory problems and a host of other ills investigators are just beginning to pinpoint and put in their proper perspective.

One of the more valuable aspects of Mr. LeCron's book is that he is convinced (as is this writer) that excessive smoking is a true addiction, ranking with drugs, sleeping pills and alcohol in difficulty of permanently effecting a cure. Withdrawal symptoms, to be sure, are not as severe, but relapses are even more frequent. This is traceable to the fact that smoking is socially acceptable, and bears no stigma. Without this stigma it is scarcely possible for unenlightened individuals to believe it can be as devastating in the long run as any addiction known to science. Because the individual can function—no matter how far below his potential —he is inclined to think cigarette smoking is an innocuous diversion, whereas the truth is far more serious.

It is slowly being recognized that smoking may kill or incapacitate its victim before some of the more spectacular addictions because it has no legal complications and can be practiced at will and even with approbation because of misleading advertising which would have us believe that cigarette smoking is a prerequisite to membership in the smart set.

In this greatly needed book, Mr. LeCron quickly disposes of the theory (encouraged by some of our leading psychiatrists) that a few cigarettes a day are to be preferred to the anxiety and tension which are presumed to increase when they are cut out entirely. In reality, each cigarette lessens the period of relief, and more and more cigarettes are required to maintain composure. The myth of smoking as a therapeutic aid in the cases of certain individuals needed exploding and it is to be hoped that some physicians will heed Mr. LeCron's advice.

It is my unshakable conviction also that individuals who

seek to counteract stress by an increased consumption of cigarettes immeasurably increase the very symptoms they seek to alleviate. It is a vicious circle of distressing affects that can be ameliorated only by abstention from the root cause—tobacco.

The technical and practical experience that Mr. LeCron brought to this book is formidable. A psychologist himself, he has for many years headed a seminar which has acquainted physicians with a modality that has thus far been too lightly considered by medical schools. He has done a great deal of original and important research and his definitive scale (worked out with Dr. Jean Bordeaux) has long been one of the two most exact methods of determining hypnotic trance depth in patients.

In regard to the techniques detailed in this book for stopping smoking, it is unnecessary to comment at great length. Mr. LeCron has treated thousands of patients, and it is his considered opinion that the techniques he has incorporated have been most successful in attaining self-hypnosis and permanently stopping smoking for those who will scrupulously follow every suggestion.

With cigarette smoking now admittedly a serious hazard to health despite the hue and cry of the tobacco interests, this book may well contain the most important advice regarding health you may ever encounter. You would do well to follow it for some of the side effects of smoking preclude a second chance.

In brief, what I am trying to say is that Mr. LeCron has written a very valuable book. The subject matter is grave and should be treated with equal gravity. Still the overall effect of this book should be hope. No matter how many times you have failed in the past, you can stop smoking. An absolutely certain method is contained between these covers.

This knowledge should make you feel better already.

Melvin Powers
Publisher

12015 Sherman Road
No. Hollywood, California 91605

Foreword

     With the report of the Surgeon General's Committee on smoking summarizing all the adverse reports of research on smoking and health, the timeliness of a book teaching how to stop smoking by using self-hypnosis needs no comment. Having such a book written by Leslie M. LeCron, one of the world's leading authorities on the subject of hypnosis, does indeed merit a great deal of comment.

     Mr. LeCron, a practicing Clinical Psychologist and the man who has taught thousands of physicians and dentists the value of the scientific use of hypnosis in medicine and dentistry, can indeed speak with authority on this subject.

     Since most individuals are completely unfamiliar with the many and varied uses of Clinical Hypnosis, and most of their knowledge is likely to be erroneous, it might be of some value to clarify a few of these misconceptions for the reader before he begins the text of LeCron's excellent book.

     Self-hypnosis can be safely used as a means of quitting smoking, as it is used to help overcome many other problems. Few realize that an individual automatically slips into a state of hypnosis many times a day. Daydreaming, which is self-hypnosis, can be observed whenever one has a need or desire to leave the reality situation temporarily.

Much has been said by the uninformed about the dangers of hypnosis and self-hypnosis. In my experience and in the experience of the many other physicians of my acquaintance who use and teach these techniques, these dangers are non-existent. It is true that the pre-psychotic should not be treated by hypnotic techniques except under carefully controlled conditions and by a well-trained psychotherapist, however, this book is not intended to be used by such individuals, nor is it intended to be used for any purpose but to help the smoker overcome his problem.

By using self-hypnosis, the subject is able to make the appropriate suggestions as outlined in this text, feeling perfectly free to do so, knowing that these suggestions will work specifically on the problem at hand.

One occasionally hears that if one stops smoking, another habit, possibly much more undesirable, will surely take its place. This too is completely untrue. It would be analogous to failing to remove an infected appendix for fear another infection must surely occur elsewhere.

Nicotine is described in the pharmacological literature as a drug that is habituating, but not addicting. I have been guilty of passing on this information in some of my writings and lectures, as have many other medical writers.

The difference in the two categories of drugs is based on the fact that addicting drugs cause the development of definite withdrawal symptoms when the drug is withheld. Having just recently become an "ex-smoker," by following the methods which LeCron gives in this book, I have most definitely changed my opinion as to the effects of nicotine on the human body. Nicotine certainly is an addicting drug, in that there *are* withdrawal symptoms when cigarettes are abruptly stopped. I feel quite sure that the intensity of these symptoms varies from one individual to the next, but this, of course, is true of any symptom complex.

There is no intention to imply that the withdrawal symptoms from nicotine are in any way comparable to the severity of those experienced by patients who are in the process of giving up the narcotic drugs such as morphine, heroin, etc., in that these people have forty-eight to seventy-two hours of sheer hell while "kicking the habit cold turkey." The nicotine withdrawal symptoms are never severe enough to produce actual physical incapacitation.

Before personally going through the experience of stopping smoking, I made the mistake of telling patients that these symptoms would not occur. In many instances this suggestion did work, and the symptoms were not experienced. However, many patients failed to quit because the symptoms did occur and, although not severe, were unexpected, and hence discouraging enough to make the individual lose faith.

Now I've learned that most people will experience mild symptoms, and I prepare them in advance, so that they are not taken by surprise. In this way they are able to cope with the withdrawal difficulties successfully. With some determination these hurdles can be readily overcome.

The method outlined in this book, using self-hypnosis, will very definitely minimize these symptoms. However, even with this help, there is still the need of strong determination and a definite desire to end the habit—to quit smoking.

The text mentions the periods of possible relapse, i.e., when one is likely to begin thinking, "I wonder what one would taste like?" Avoiding this pitfall by being prepared for it is vitally important.

All in all, with the help of this book, stopping smoking

should be much easier, surprisingly so for most smokers,
even the heavy smoker and the addict. Mr. LeCron and
the publishers deserve thanks for contributing a great deal
to lessening the danger of cancer.

RAY LaScola, M.D.

Santa Monica, Calif.

How This Book Can Help
You Stop Smoking

If you are starting to read this book presumably you are a cigarette smoker. Probably you are toying with the idea of quitting but are doubtful as to whether you can break the habit. Possibly you are like Mark Twain who quipped, "It's easy to quit smoking. I've done it many, many times."

Almost any cigarette smoker who has read the report of the Surgeon General's Advisory Committee on Smoking has shuddered at the thought of developing lung cancer or some circulatory or respiratory ailment as the result of his habit. He has also quailed at the thought of trying to quit! Fear can be a great incentive towards wanting to "kick" the habit, but probably no very large percentage of the millions of smokers will actually quit permanently. Those who do will mainly be the ones least likely to have their health affected.

Why is it true that no large number will discard their "coffin nails"? Such a report should make anyone realize that cigarette smoking often is detrimental to health. It would seem that any sensible, intelligent person would immediately stop smoking. But bankruptcy of the tobacco companies is unlikely. If you have ever tried to stop, and are a fairly heavy smoker, you know the answer. Usually it's a most unpleasant, very difficult matter to break the habit. This is particularly true if you are a real addict, and many smokers are definitely addicted. Some light smokers find it fairly easy to stop. Heavier smokers find it a horrible experience and usually fail.

You can stop smoking.

Is there any method of stopping that will work successfully without the usual unpleasant withdrawal symptoms? There certainly is such a method and one rather easily learned. True, it is not a magic wand which can be waved so all desire for a cigarette instantly vanishes, but it can make the quitting process relatively easy. For many it will be almost like the magic wand. The method can also be applied to many other detrimental conditions as well as to smoking.

As a psychologist often called on to help someone stop smoking I have studied this matter of the cigarette habit rather intensely. I've talked to many who have stopped successfully without help. I've helped many others with the method given here. Some have had no difficulty at all. Others have had a little trouble but have found it relatively easy. A few have failed for reasons which will be described, not having followed out the method fully.

How self-hypnosis helps.

One of the main reasons for the success of this technique is the use of self-hypnosis in connection with it. Lest the idea of hypnosis seem frightening, let me say that I have yet to hear of anyone ever having any bad results from its use. Scores of thousands of women have gone through childbirth with hypnosis and many thousands of people have been treated with hypnotherapy.

Many people are afraid of hypnosis due to misconceptions and entirely false ideas about it. Many physicians are entirely uninformed about hypnosis and have these same misconceptions. They will be explained and these false ideas corrected in a later chapter. With a correct understanding about it you'll have no fear about its use.

Perhaps the best reassurance as to possible dangers in hypnosis is to tell you that you've been self-hypnotized literally hundreds or even thousands of times, depending on your age. It is a common and quite normal occurrence with all of us.

You're hypnotized daily.

Everyone slips spontaneously into hypnosis every day of his life, often repeatedly. Do you ever daydream? Everyone does and daydreaming is nothing but self-induced hypnosis. When you become absorbed in anything you do, such as reading a book, studying, listening to a lecture, watching a TV program, carrying on your work, you slip into hypnosis. It happens whenever you concentrate intently. These situations are not labeled hypnosis, but that's what they are. Many religious ceremonies tend to produce it in those who attend, particularly if there is music, chanting and ritual.

Realizing how such a trance state develops so commonly, you should have no fears about hypnotizing yourself. There's nothing mysterious or mystical about it. You will be doing intentionally what has resulted spontaneously with you many, many times. Of course you had no bad effects from these experiences. If you know the signs of a trance state, and I'll tell you about them later, and look for them, you'll often notice your friends, and members of your family, in such a state. I have a young son and often observed him self-hypnotized even before he was a year old.

Can you learn to induce self-hypnosis? Not everyone can, but a large majority can learn it readily with the ways given here to help you. You'll find it a very valuable ability in many ways. It can be used to overcome detrimental character traits, habits, personality difficulties, and even some emotional (psychosomatic) illnesses. I've written of methods of doing this in a previous book, *Self-Hypnotism: The Technique and Its Use in Daily Living* (Prentice-Hall, Englewood Cliffs, New Jersey).

Even if you should find yourself to be one of the few who cannot induce hypnosis in yourself, the methods and techniques which will be described will be a great help in stopping smoking. They will be more effective with self-hypnosis, but that is not essential for success.

To stop—you must know why you started.

One important factor in overcoming the cigarette habit is learning why you smoke—why it is compulsive if that is true with you. When you have insight into causes and motivations, it is much easier to end the habit. Some of these are easily recognized. Others may be deep-seated psychological motivations working in the subconscious part of your mind, so strong that they must be overcome in order for you to be successful in stopping smoking. This may be why so many are unable to stop, no matter how much they may want to, or how hard they try. These motivations are partly responsible for the very unpleasant symptoms often experienced when one has stopped smoking. With such motivations understood and removed, these symptoms are either not a problem at all, or are only very mild.

How Cary Grant did it.

The methods given here to help the smoker break away have been taught to hundreds of physicians who have attended courses in hypnotic techniques given by HYPNOSIS SYMPOSIUMS,—I'm one of the instructors with this group. Thousands of people have been successful in ending the smoking habit with these methods. You can join their number when you apply the methods.

Cary Grant, famous motion picture star, has told in interviews of how he used these methods. He was a very heavy smoker for years. He had heard that hypnosis could be most helpful in quitting. Grant purchased a copy of my book *Hypnotism Today* (written with Dr. Jean Bordeaux—Grune & Stratton, New York). In it is a sample "induction talk." He had his wife read this to him. He happened to be an excellent hypnotic subject and became deeply hypnotized. Then his wife gave him suggestions aimed at removing the desire to smoke and to overcome the habit. Grant reports that subsequently he found all desire had left and he was able to stop with no withdrawal symptoms and no difficulty.

Grant's case isn't typical, though many others have had similar results. More often there is difficulty for a few days, but with determination and the methods given here using self-hypnosis, it is easy to become an ex-smoker.

Not every smoker wants to quit. Some prefer to keep on regardless of possible harmful effects. Some would like to cut down on the number of cigarettes smoked, feeling that a moderate amount of smoking is unlikely to do any damage. It is indeed possible to curtail smoking, and a program is given for this as well as for eliminating the tobacco habit entirely. Whether you wish to become an ex-smoker or merely to cut your consumption of cigarettes to a more moderate quantity, self-hypnosis is the most effective tool to employ, in connection with the various other techniques described in the text.

LESLIE M. LeCRON

Contents

1

What Type of Smoker
Are You?

Before giving you a program to follow in order to stop smoking, let us consider the tobacco habit and your own particular case. Individuals vary a good deal in their patterns. Some smoke cigars, others pipes, but we are mainly concerned with the cigarette smoker.

Pipe and cigar smokers.

Since publication of the Surgeon General's Committee report, tobacco dealers have noted an increased sale of cigars and particularly of pipes. According to the report, they are not greatly involved in causing lung cancer and other diseases. Evidently many who do not want to give up smoking, or who feel that they can't, are trying to substitute one of these forms of smoking.

The main enjoyment from cigarette smoking is from inhaling. Most pipe and cigar smokers do not inhale as the tobacco is too strong. Whether or not changing your form of smoking will end the chances of your health being affected is doubtful. It may be out of the frying pan into the fire. If you do change and continue to inhale, the damage would be greater than with cigarettes. You may find the change unsatisfactory for you if you do not inhale. Furthermore, cigar and pipe smoking has been found to have a tendency to cause lip cancer.

There seems to be something of a ritual involved in pipe smoking. Fussing over the pipe itself, preparing the tobacco, pressing it carefully into the pipe with just the right tamping-down, lighting and keeping it lit, scraping out the residue, and cleaning the pipe are a part of the ritual. There is also a feeling of masculinity experienced, for the ladies do not go in for pipe smoking.

Neither does the gentler sex find cigar smoking enjoyable. This too is a sign of masculinity, indicating the businessman and executive type. Although there are some exceptions, most pipe and cigar smokers would fall into a classification as being light smokers. Most could stop with little or no difficulty, if they so wished.

You may change to this type of smoking and find it satisfying your needs. However, most who try to make the change will find themselves back on cigarettes within a few days, in all probability.

The cigarette smoker who smokes lightly.

Cigarette smokers fall into four classes. If you smoke less than a pack a day you certainly are not an addict. If you smoke less than fifteen cigarettes a day, almost certainly you can quit without much trouble. There would be no withdrawal symptoms. Yet even the light smoker has developed a habit. Some might break it with only the decision to stop, but more likely it will not be quite that easy. A modification of the techniques given in this book will certainly help, though some would be unnecessary.

The medium smoker.

Probably about half of all cigarette smokers will fall into the classification of medium smokers. This type will smoke a pack or perhaps a pack and a half each day. Such a person enjoys smoking. Up to the time when he has read reports of the possible health dangers in smoking, he has given little thought to its bad aspects. He may have thought vaguely at times of stopping. When the dangers are called to his attention, he may be motivated to quit.

The quitting process is usually not too hard for this type of smoker. He has some trouble the first few days, but by exerting plenty of so called will-power (or rather "won't power") he does stop. In the past, finding that he can stop, he often has started again and boasts that he can quit any time but does not want to quit. Realizing the possible serious consequences of continued smoking, he will find our method very easy and probably will never start smoking again.

The heavy smoker.

The heavy smoker is one who consumes more than a pack and a half a day, often three or even more. He knows he smokes too much, knows he should quit. He has vague plans of doing this "someday" but rarely seems to get around to it. It's always in the future. He makes excuses, rationalizes that some people may develop lung cancer or some other illness, but it will not be he.

Perhaps he does make an effort to stop, particularly if his physician warns and scares him sufficiently. He tries. He finds it difficult and has a bad time for a couple of weeks. Probably he thinks often of how he wants a cigarette. After each meal it's a real battle to keep from smoking. He probably has some withdrawal symptoms, severe with some people, not too extreme with others. He may succeed in quitting, though many will fall by the wayside and give up.

The cigarette addict.

According to the Committee's report on smoking and health, smoking is classified as habituation rather than addiction. The usually accepted definition of addiction includes an overpowering compulsion to take the drug, with a tendency to increase the dose and both a psychological and physical dependence on the effects of the drug.

Habituation differs in that the desire to take the drug is not compulsive; there is little or no tendency to increase the dose; no physical dependence, and detrimental effects if any are primarily on the individual. With addiction, the effects involve both the individual and society.

Probably the majority of cigarette smokers are habituated rather than addicted. Nevertheless, I agree with the statement of Dr. LaScola in his foreword to this book that quite a large number of cigarette smokers are definitely addicted.

The person I would classify as an addict is a heavy smoker, though not all heavy smokers are addicted, and some addicts do not smoke very excessive quantities. He will consume at least one and a half packs a day and probably more. His smoking is more than a habit. It is compulsive. Under stress he must light one cigarette after another. They give great satisfaction, seemingly calming nerves and bringing relaxation. While this is temporarily true, nicotine is not a sedative. Actually it is a stimulant and a strong poison. Concentrated, only a small amount taken orally or intravenously would be fatal.

The addict often takes only a few puffs on a cigarette, then puts it down. A moment later he reaches for it again, may find it burned down and lights another from it. His nervousness is quieted for a moment, then tension mounts and he must smoke again to "quiet his nerves."

The addict is almost sure to wake up in the morning, coughing, hacking, and ridding himself of much phlegm, with a horrible taste in his mouth. He quickly reaches for a cigarette before dressing. He inhales deeply with a sigh of satisfaction. He smokes another cigarette as he shaves. If breakfast is delayed, he lights another. After breakfast comes the best and most enjoyable one of all, lighted almost before he has swallowed the last morsel of food.

After many more cigarettes during the morning, with coughing spells in between, cigarettes don't seem to taste as good, though the one immediately following a meal is always enjoyable. I'm doubtful if many smokers really enjoy the taste of cigarettes. It is the result of inhalation that gives satisfaction, rather than the taste of the tobacco or the smoke. The pipe or cigar smoker seems to find more enjoyment in taste.

The addict fully realizes that he smokes too much. He may even confess to being an addict. He often thinks of stopping but shies away with horror from the idea of actually quitting. If told by his physician that he should or must stop for some physical reason, he becomes panicky. If he tries, he literally goes through hellish symptoms, not like those of the alcoholic or narcotic addict, but bad enough.

Even if successful in stopping for a few days, the urge and desire for a smoke is present most of the time, strongly present. He thinks about smoking much of the time. Very few addicts ever stop permanently. One of the addict's greatest difficulties is that he knows he should stop but he cannot work himself up to the point of stopping or of actually wanting to quit.

When the addict does try to break the habit, he finds it an agonizing experience. He becomes extremely nervous, with anxiety which may become acute. He is irritable and probably takes it out on his family. His hands tremble, his hands and feet may swell (due to increased blood circulation), he perhaps perspires a good deal. He is very jittery and continually must fight the desire to smoke. He may succeed but most addicts give up after a few days of trying to stop.

Even the addict can use the methods given here and will find such symptoms greatly modified or even missing. Some few will not be able to quit even with these methods and if health needs demand quitting, should consult a psychotherapist. With such extreme addiction, until psychotherapeutic treatment has been successful, there are some contraindications for trying to stop smoking, as will be pointed out. But very few would find themselves in this situation. A few sessions with a good psychotherapist should ease the compulsion to smoke so that our techniques for tobacco habit control could then succeed fairly easily.

SUMMARY

You should be able easily to determine now in which category of smoker you fall. If you are a light smoker it will be very easy to stop with the methods which will be given. Some can be omitted by the light smoker. The medium smoker also will have no great trouble quitting. Self-hypnosis will be helpful for either the light or medium smoker.

Some heavy smokers will also find it surprisingly easy to control the habit. Even some addicts will have no great difficulty. Others will need to be very thorough in following all the techniques given. They may have some withdrawal symptoms and some difficulty but nevertheless will be successful in quitting. A very few addicts will find their compulsion too strong, so that only with psychotherapeutic treatment would it be possible to end the compulsion to smoke. Then they, too, will have little difficulty. Since such a person, smoking excessively, is most likely to have his health affected in the long run, seeking psychological help certainly is indicated.

2

Why You Smoke and What It's Costing You

Reports of the incidence of smoking among children show that most begin to smoke in the age bracket between twelve and twenty. Surprisingly about five percent of boys and only one percent of girls begin to smoke before twelve years of age. Members of the present adult generation more often began to smoke at a later age, many not until the late teens.

One of the main reasons for beginning to smoke is status striving, this in a broad sense. Some of the needs involved are to be accepted by one's friends and peers, to develop self-esteem, confidence and a suitable self-image, and to cope with feelings of inadequacy. Part of this is a striving to be adult. Probably this is the most common reason for children beginning to smoke.

Another factor may be the rebellion against authority. Few juvenile delinquents are non-smokers. Investigations show that there is a relationship between smoking practices of the parents and whether or not their children smoke. A child is much more likely to start smoking if one or both of its parents are smokers. Curiosity is another factor that may be one of the reasons for beginning to smoke.

No smoker personality has ever been found in research but some personality factors are associated with smoking. Neuroticism, extroversion, and more psychosomatic manifestations are seen in smokers.

The first few cigarettes when one begins to smoke are most unpleasant, with dizziness, nausea and vomiting as the result. It is a wonder that anyone ever continues after finding the first cigarettes so unpleasant. But this soon ends and the habit of smoking quickly develops.

Why we smoke—the oral need.

Aside from the motives involved in beginning to smoke, what are those which lead us to continue to smoke? Freud theorized that we all pass through certain stages in the process of maturing and developing. He called the earliest one the oral stage, this immediately following birth. Many people never seem to grow completely out of this stage and unconsciously continue to need much oral satisfaction.

It has been mentioned previously that cigarette smoking is the equivalent of the thumb-sucking of childhood and both stem from nursing as an infant. Having something in the mouth serves to satisfy this oral need. Other detrimental ways of satisfying it are overeating, with resulting obesity, and alcoholism. Both are likely to be far more detrimental to health than is smoking. Overeating is a problem with millions of people.

One of the problems in controlling the tobacco habit is to contend with this oral need or craving, either modifying or ending it. At first we use some substitute for cigarettes, then after a short time we try to make the substitute unnecessary. An understanding of the subconscious mind and how best to influence it aids in establishing this control of oral needs.

The need to do something with our hands.

When we smoke we are not only satisfying this oral need, but we may also be satisfying a need to do something with our hands. This seems to be a part of nervous tension, and modern living tends to produce nervous tension in all of us in varying degree. The more nervous you are, the more you seem to want to do something with your hands. Gesturing is one outlet. The Chinese have been reported to sometimes carry a little stick about—a "twiddlestick"—which is twiddled between the fingers. Tibetans make similar use of a prayer wheel which they twirl much of the time. Telling beads or a rosary is along the same line.

Smoking and nervous tension.

Smoking is very largely regarded as a means of relieving nervous tension, quieting the nerves, which it seems to do temporarily. Then you become more nervous. This is one area where hypnosis is of great value. You can learn with it to discharge or relieve nervous tension to a surprising degree. While hypnotized you are extremely relaxed and you learn to remain more relaxed and freer of tension. Then you do not need to relieve it by smoking.

Many people lack self-confidence and are uncomfortable when in a social group. They feel self-conscious and smoking seems to relieve this feeling to some extent. It adds to sociability.

Emotional problems invariably cause an increase in

tension, and who doesn't sometimes have an emotional problem? More tension, more smoking. But with better relaxation through hypnosis, you won't develop as much tension and nervousness. Even if you should be one of the few who can't seem to learn self-hypnosis, you'll probably relax better as you try to become hypnotized.

How tobacco advertising affects us.

It is likely that the government will undertake to control the advertising of the tobacco companies with their implied message that smoking is good for you. Athletic heroes sometimes deliver this data, of course stressing the value and delight found in smoking the particular brand of cigarette being advertised. The athlete is paid for his statements and may even be a non-smoker himself. Most top athletes do not smoke because they know smoking affects their wind and cuts energy.

Advertising is a matter of suggestion and we are all suggestible. The delights of smoking are pictured in TV commercials and by the printed word. Suggestions such as "reach for a cigarette" are pounded at us. The tobacco industry spent $75,000,000.00 in a recent year for television advertising and this is only about a fourth of the total advertising expense for these companies. You can bet it produced results or such expense would quickly be discontinued.

Advertising is suggestion and is aimed at influencing your subconscious mind. This fails if you consciously analyze the TV commercials you see and hear. Listen attentively and watch. Pay attention to the details and the statements made. You'll quickly note how lacking in sense it is in many respects. You'll not be influenced if you do this every time a tobacco commercial flashes on your TV screen.

Your children are copycats.

If you have children this can be a great incentive to stop smoking. Did your father smoke? That may be one of the reasons why you began to smoke. Nowadays mother may also be a smoker, making the situation even stronger for the child. Children tend to imitate their parents. In psychology this is called *identification*. They want to be like the parents. If mama is obese, her child is very likely to grow up as a fatty. We all tend at times to identify with those close to us. Identification means dramatization. This may be carried out to an extent where we not only assume our parents' character traits but even an illness from which a parent suffers.

As an example of identification, I once had a patient who came to me with an itching ear. He continually scratched it by inserting his little finger in it and jiggling the finger. The itch had persisted for years but doctors could find no physical reason for it. While working with this patient I asked if anyone in his family had ever had such an itching ear.

"Oh yes," he answered. "My mother was always scratching her ear in that way. She was slightly deaf in it, too, and I notice I've been getting a bit deaf as I get older." This was merely a matter of identification. He was very fond of his mother and was dramatizing her pattern. When he realized this, his ear stopped itching.

You certainly do not want your children to identify with you as to smoking. This can serve as a very good incentive for you to stop.

Some other reasons for you to end the tobacco habit.

To make your program of quitting the tobacco habit effective, your motivations must be understood and must be strong. This helps influence your subconscious mind so it aids you in quitting. These motives must arouse a real desire to rid yourself of this infernal "Old Man of the Mountain who is riding on your shoulders." Motivation is of the utmost importance, so we will go into all aspects very thoroughly.

Health is your most important reason for stopping smoking.

Of course you wish to stay healthy. The harmful effect of cigarette smoking on health should be your main reason for wanting to quit. Unfortunately it's easy to rationalize and think that it will be someone else, not ourselves, who will develop some bad illness from smoking. If you've smoked for several years without bad results, you may think it will never happen to you. But the illnesses resulting from cigarette smoking usually appear following many years of smoking. Sometimes it is more quickly, for this is only a general statement. A bad heart could give out any time.

In the next chapter the Committee's findings on smoking and health will be considered at some length.

Nicotine and its effect.

Nicotine is a deadly poison, although not enough is absorbed from smoking to actually poison one. Nevertheless there is an accumulation in the system of the drug.

It's partly due to the effect of nicotine and partly psychological when withdrawal symptoms develop after the heavy smoker breaks off and stops smoking. After quitting, it takes about a week for all the nicotine to have been thrown out of the system.

There is a drug, lobeline sulphate, which acts as a substitute for nicotine, tending to lessen the craving for nicotine. It is sold under various trade names and doesn't require a prescription. Advertisers make great claims for their product, leading you to believe that all you need do is take a few of these pills or lozenges and you'll lose all desire to smoke. In fact, there is very little effect noticed from the drug, though it may be of some slight help in your quitting program.

Rather surprisingly, the Committee's report on smoking does not blame nicotine itself as being much of a factor in causing the illnesses resulting from smoking. But it is a big factor in the quitting process.

There are other substances in cigarettes and tobacco that are harmful to health, such as tars, gases, and still others. Not too much is known about them though research is being conducted to find out more about their effects and possible ways of eliminating any of these substances found to be harmful. Filters have very little effect in preventing them from being absorbed.

It's expensive to smoke.

The average smoker burns up a little more than one pack a day. With national, state, and sometimes even local taxes, the average cost is about twenty-eight cents a pack. It doesn't seem like much when you buy a pack, but what about the cumulative cost? It amounts to $102.00 a year. In ten years it's over a thousand dollars. If you smoked for fifty years it would amount to over $5000.00. A nice amount to have all in one lump sum, but you would have burned it up. Double these figures for the two-pack-a-day smoker.

In one year some seventy million Americans bought 523 billion cigarettes! The tobacco business runs to eight billion dollars a year. That's big business. It includes all the farmers who raise tobacco, mostly in southern states. So any regulation of this industry enters the political field. Southern legislators can be counted on to fight controls, even at the expense of the nation's health. However, the government is planning to curb advertising claims of the tobacco companies and to stage a long campaign of education of the rising generation. It is hoped that this will gradually cut the sale of cigarettes.

Probably a sudden great loss in sales of cigarettes would be economically damaging to the south, but if gradual, farmers can readily turn to other crops without loss, factories to the making of other products.

Smoking is a nasty habit.

Though you yourself are not aware of it, smoking causes unpleasant breath. Your spouse knows it does! You have dirty ash trays around the house, messy clothes where ashes have fallen on them, stained fingers. When you are free of all this, you'll be much cleaner and more comfortable.

Ashes may be good for keeping out moths but they do not do much good for carpets or clothing in other ways. Have you ever dropped a cigarette or had one fall unnoticed from an ash tray so a piece of furniture was burned? Or have you knocked the spark from a cigarette without realizing it, and burned a hole in your clothing, perhaps also in your hide? I'll bet you have. Not long ago it cost me a good sum to have a dining room table refinished because of a bad burn.

If you add up all the incidental expense of smoking, such as for burned furniture and clothing, cleaning of clothing, etc., it would make another large expense over the course of the years. When you have stopped smoking, you'll be saving money which will come in very handy in other ways.

Accomplishment is enjoyable.

Another good motive for ending the tobacco habit is the pleasure gained from accomplishment. It bolsters one's ego. When you've stopped smoking you can feel that it's a real accomplishment. It's something you can boast about to your friends, while patting yourself on the back. You can even gloat a bit and feel very virtuous. You'll probably make yourself very obnoxious to your friends, but they'll be envying you and giving you respect.

Some other advantages in breaking away from the cigarette habit.

Physically, when you stop smoking your appearance will improve. Your skin will be clearer, your teeth cleaner and whiter, your mouth free of that horrible dark brown taste, your breath fresh. You'll be sleeping better, having more energy, and your mind will be working more efficiently. How good it will seem not to waken in the morning hacking and coughing, finding you can climb steps without wheezing and snorting. All these are the eventual rewards which come within a short time after E-day. (Emancipation day.) You'll probably notice still others after a time.

What about cutting down.

In spite of all the reasons why one should stop smoking there is another side to the picture which must be considered. Many smokers get a great deal of satisfaction from smoking and it is an important matter to gain this satisfaction. The advantages and benefits from foregoing cigarettes may not be enough to counterbalance the enjoyment found in smoking. The motives for stopping are not strong enough to make such a person want to stop. Perhaps he would admit that it would be better for him to stop, but he has no desire to stop. He dismisses any thought of smoking affecting his health as most unlikely. After all, many who smoke all their lives escape the illnesses which sometimes come from smoking.

Such a person may realize that it would be wise for him to curtail his smoking, if it is excessive. He can see the sense in this. Cutting down certainly will decrease any slight possibility of developing some illness. Other motivations for cutting down will be similar to those for stopping completely but will not be as strongly felt.

Another consideration to be given as to cutting down is the possible difficulty of stopping altogether. Perhaps, or even probably, it would not be possible to stop, or it might be entirely too unpleasant to go through with any such attempt. It should be much easier to modify his smoking need and he will feel that this can be accomplished. By cutting down, the enjoyment and satisfaction found in smoking can be continued, with the risks and disadvantages minimized.

Reasoning such as this is likely to cause many smokers to prefer this as a goal rather than to stop smoking. A workable program will be given for accomplishing this.

SUMMARY

Smoking is first begun for a variety of complicated reasons. Probably the main one is status seeking, with the desire to be adult. There may be a revolt from authority in some cases. Most smokers have an oral need which smoking satisfies, this being related to the thumb-sucking of childhood and to nursing in infancy. Overeating and overdrinking also are other ways of satisfying this oral craving. Cigarette smoking may also serve to satisfy a need to be doing something with our hands. Smoking seems to relieve nervous tension, although this effect is only temporary, for nicotine is a stimulant and not a sedative.

There are many good reasons for you to decide to stop smoking, or at least to cut down if you prefer not to stop entirely. Of course health is the most important one. Another is to set your children an example so that they do not imitate you and take up smoking. The cost of the tobacco habit is considerable when you consider it over a period of time. And smoking really is a nasty habit.

Nicotine itself does not seem to be very harmful to health and it is some of the many other substances in tobacco which cause illnesses. Nicotine does accumulate in the system, however, and a physical craving develops which with many of us will cause withdrawal symptoms when we stop smoking.

3

What the Surgeon General's
Committee on Smoking Reported

If you are more than a light smoker, then you are sure to have a hard time trying to stop smoking unless you have a strong desire to end the tobacco habit. Your motives are of the utmost importance and therefore they should be stressed so your wish to rid yourself of the habit will be very strong. Nothing will be of more help to you in your program.

Of course your health is important to you and is a prime consideration in your decision to quit smoking. No one wants to develop any illness, particularly such a horrible disease as lung cancer. Unfortunately, it's rather a natural tendency to think that it might happen to someone else but surely it won't happen to you.

I've always been blessed with excellent health myself. Two years ago I developed a broken appendix and had to have surgery. When the doctors told me I must have the appendix out at once, I was shocked. I'd never had an operation. I remember the indignation I felt. *I* wasn't supposed to have such a condition! It just didn't seem right. Similarly, we are like the ostrich and want to bury our head in the sand when we think of smoking affecting our health. It could be someone else—not me!

Over the past few years a good many research projects as to the physical effects of smoking have been carried out by the medical profession. There were some conflicting reports but most were definitely adverse. Cigarettes particularly do cause disease. Finally the British government took official action, staging a campaign to warn the British public of the situation. Tobacco sales promptly fell off greatly in that country. Latest reports are that they have come back and are about the same as before.

The Surgeon General's Committee.

In the United States a ten-man committee of doctors was appointed to look into the facts and weigh the case against tobacco. The members were all prominent physicians and their appointment was approved by the tobacco companies. These medical men were from various fields, pathology, biochemistry, surgery, pharmacology, internal medicine, etc. They investigated some 8000 different studies of the effect of cigarette smoking on health, including tests on the effect of tobacco on animals.

These tests seem to indicate surprisingly that nicotine itself is rather harmless. It is other ingredients of cigarettes that do the damage, such as tars and gases. Pipe and cigar smoking is much less risky, although with such smokers lip cancer cases do show an increase so this type of smoking is not entirely innocent of harm.

One of the most extensive and important research studies considered by the Committee was a survey made by Dr. E. Cuyler Hammond, who is chief statistician of the American Cancer Society. This study is still unfinished. The statistics gathered were analyzed by the use of computers. Some 422,000 male Americans were surveyed, aged from 40 to 89, and all types included. While the death rate ran about twice as high for medium or heavy smokers as for non-smokers, the lung cancer death rate was about nine times as high. If you are a medium or heavy smoker, the chances are then nine times as great for you to die from lung cancer as for the non-smoker to end with this terrible disease. It should make you think and should serve as the strongest possible motive for bringing you into the ex-smoker class. Many other research projects show about the same results as does Dr. Hammond's.

With the report of the committee, which was made in January, 1964, there can no longer be any doubt of the fact that cigarette smoking is definitely a large factor in causing lung cancer, bronchitis, emphysema, and heart disease. Most impressive statistics are given.

What about filtertips?

Cigarette manufacturers make many claims about filtertips, but the report was neutral on this question. Some gases and tars probably are removed by filters, but there is no indication that they are of great value, despite claims, especially since so little is known about the substances which are harmful. Claims are also made as to the safety of de-nicotinized cigarettes but actually there is no such thing. It is impossible to remove much of the nicotine from the tobacco.

Can suggestion cause disease?

Many physicians and others who are authorities on suggestion and hypnosis feel that suggestion definitely can be a cause for some diseases. Scientifically this would be hard to prove. It is only a matter of opinion, which I certainly share. For instance, the statistics on deaths from heart conditions show a very great increase of such deaths in the course of the past few years. This is also true of various other diseases, with no reason for it being apparent.

During this period the medical profession, through magazine and newspaper articles and by word of mouth from physicians, has impressed on the general public the need for physical checkup, particularly as to the heart. Much attention was called to cardiac disease and to still others. If you are afraid of some disease and think about it much, it is quite possible that anticipation may bring it on. It would not be surprising if the furor over the dangers in cigarette smoking actually may serve to increase still more the incidence of lung cancer and the pulmonary ailments which smoking tends to produce. I believe there may be a sudden and rather large increase in such statistics over the next two or three years, even though many of us will have stopped smoking, which should instead bring down the statistical incidence.

All this should make you think.

Learning the results of this Committee's report can only make any intelligent person reach the conclusion that he should stop smoking cigarettes. Believing you should stop is not enough. You must develop a strong desire to stop. Thinking you should but not wanting to stop sets up a conflict and makes the quitting process a tough one. One of our main objectives here is to develop the strongest possible wish to be free of the habit, and a determination to accomplish this freedom. Fears and intelligent consideration of the problem will stimulate such desire, and ways of still further developing it will be discussed. When you follow the steps given later on, you will almost certainly want to be an ex-smoker. Then it is easy or at least relatively easy.

A summary of the findings reported by the Committee.

So that you may know the conditions found to be caused or related to cigarette smoking, they are listed here as taken from the published report.

Cigarette smoking definitely causes lung cancer and the risk increases with duration of smoking and the number of cigarettes smoked. This may also cause cancer of the larynx, and possibly of the esophagus and the bladder.

It is the most important cause of chronic bronchitis, and there is a relationship also with pulmonary emphysema. Cough and sputum production is greatly increased, as is breathlessness. There is a moderately increased risk of death from influenza and pneumonia. Cigarette smoking does not seem to cause asthma.

Male cigarette smokers have a higher death rate from coronary artery disease than non-smoker males. Incidence of peptic ulcer is indicated, and there is increased mortality from cirrhosis of the liver.

Women who smoke cigarettes during pregnancy tend to have babies of lower birth weight.

Smoking is associated with accidental deaths from fires.

These are the conclusions reached by the Committee after a most exhaustive study of the problem and the investigations carried out by various researchers.

4

How Your Inner Mind
Helps You

Most everyone knows that there is an inner part of the mind, which has been given various different names—subconscious, unconscious, subjective, subliminal, the id and various other terms. In psychiatry the most commonly accepted designation is "unconscious." Freud called it the id. But unconscious has two meanings, the inner mind being one. It also means a period of unconsciousness, as in sleep, under an anesthetic drug or when knocked out. Also, the inner part of the mind is not unconscious. It is very much aware, even more so than the conscious part. Hence "subconscious" will be used here as more descriptive and preferable.

It is a good thing for us to know something about that part of the mind. It controls your compulsive impulses, and some of your motivations in smoking are at an unconscious level. Unfortunately we still know little about the actual make-up of this part of the mind, or the way it works. The more we know about it the easier it will be to influence it—best done through hypnosis. And influencing it will be of the utmost value in helping you stop smoking.

Even the old Greek physicians Hippocrates and Aesculapius were aware of this part of our mental makeup. In modern times Sigmund Freud advanced our knowledge about it tremendously with his research into subconscious processes and with his psychoanalytic concepts. Strangely, there has been little further research of any importance since his day. This is remarkable because it is now well recognized that much illness is emotionally caused—psychosomatic ailments. Some physicians think about half of all illness falls in this category; others claim 80%. Dr. Hans Selye, a Canadian authority, believes stress is involved in all illness, even infectious ones, because stress lowers our resistances so we become open to infections.

In the United States and in somewhat less extent in the other English-speaking countries Freudian ideas are taught in all medical schools and other psychiatric training centers. Hence most psychiatrists accept them, at least in modified form. In all other parts of the world Freud is largely disregarded and the ideas of the great Russian physiologist Pavlov are favored. These theories will be described later.

How your inner mind functions.

The Freudian view of the makeup of the inner mind is undoubtedly correct in some aspects but it fails to account for all its operations. On the whole it describes it in too mechanical a way. Freud believed that the mind as a whole consists of three main divisions. The part we think and reason with, our awareness, he called the ego. Another part, best thought of as our conscience, he termed the superego. Below consciousness is a part he called the id, it being the seat of memory and of our basic instincts. Later he theorized of another part lying between the id and the ego, just below the level of awareness, and called it the preconscious. The term subconscious as used in this book would include the id, preconscious, and the superego.

Dr. Carl Jung, famous Swiss psychiatrist, believed the superego is not just conscience but is the most spiritual part of us. He termed it the superconscious mind. Jung believed it a part of a universal mind, directly connected with God—a part of the Supreme Being. He adopted this from some of the Oriental philosophies.

Automatic writing.

The late Anita Mühl, a leading woman psychiatrist, experimented with automatic writing in trying to learn more about the subconscious mind. This is a fascinating phenomenon. If you hold a pen or soft pencil in your hand, the subconscious can control the muscles of your hand and arm and can write intelligibly without your being aware of what is being written. You can read a book or magazine while the hand is busily writing. Interestingly, a few "automats" have been able to read with the conscious mind while the right hand writes on some subject. At the same time the left hand writes about something entirely different. Thus there are three different mental activities taking place at once! You may have played with a Ouija board or seen one. The subconscious mind causes your hand to move it, and this is just a variation of automatic writing.

Dr. Mühl claimed that four out of five people can learn to write automatically, although several hours of training might be needed to learn it. Others have found the percentage much less. Almost any good hypnotic subject can do this while in hypnosis. If you doodle, it is the same type of activity and doodlers can usually learn automatic writing readily. Your doodling may be quite meaningful if you could interpret it.

In experimenting with fifty different subjects, Dr. Mühl was able to secure automatic writing from seven different levels of the subconscious, each identifying itself in some way. These ranged, she reported, from a part corresponding to Jung's superconscious to the lowest level of the mind which would identify itself as the "old Nick" or the "Devil" in us. It seems to be a part containing our basic drives and instincts—our caveman attitudes.

The subconscious as a mechanical computer.

Still another theory of the make-up of the inner mind has been described by Dr. Maxwell Maltz (*Psychocybernetics*, Prentice-Hall, Englewood Cliffs, N.J.), though Norbert Weiner was the first to advance this idea. It is that the subconscious works very much as does an electric computer, acting through the brain. It is purely mechanistic, and so complicated that the most elaborate computer would be a toy in comparison. This theory would seem to doubt the ability of the inner mind to reason.

Some psychologists, the behaviorists, have denied the existence of a subconscious mind, believing that we are entirely controlled by our conditioning and what has happened to us—that all our behavior and thinking is purely mechanical. This idea no longer has acceptance by present-day psychologists. It is easily refuted by the fact that automatic writing can be produced which definitely shows the existence of an inner part of the mind which thinks and reasons.

There is no doubt that the subconscious performs mechanistically but theories must also take into consideration its ability to reason and think. It has been said, and it is undoubtedly true, that this part of the mind only reasons deductively, while the conscious part reasons both deductively and inductively. The fact that the inner mind reasons can also be demonstrated by means of subconsciously controlled movements made as signals in answer to questions worded so they can be answered *yes* or *no.*

Subconscious control of the mechanism of the body.

One of the duties of the subconscious is the control of body processes, functioning through the brain. It is something like a thermostat. A part of the brain regulates the autonomic nervous system and through it controls all the organs and glands. Probably the subconscious also controls the chemical and electrical reactions of the body also. Experiments with hypnosis have been made which definitely prove scientifically these controls, changes occurring as the result of suggestions.

By hypnotic suggestion the circulation of the blood can be controlled, heart-beat either slowed or speeded up, the action of organs and glands changed, the rate of healing of a wound or injury greatly increased, body temperature raised or lowered. Many other bodily changes can be caused to take place through hypnotic suggestion.

How the subconscious reasons and thinks.

If we wish to influence the inner mind, as will be one of your purposes in ending the cigarette habit, it is important to know the way it works. At times it seems to be quite childish and immature. It takes everything entirely literally. Often we do not say what we mean; a matter of semantics. For instance, a commonly used phrase is "that makes me mad." We intend to say we are angry, but we actually have said we have become insane.

With a person in hypnosis, the subconscious seems to be nearer the surface, or in a very deep state it may have largely taken over conscious thinking. If a person in the waking state is asked the question, "Would you tell me where you were born?" he will invariably name the place. He interprets the question as a desire to know the location. In a fairly deep state of hypnosis the person would reply by saying "yes" or more likely would merely nod his head. That is the correct literal answer to the question. Yes, he is willing to tell you. This is a good example of how the subconscious will take things literally.

Sometimes a detrimental situation arises from this literalness of the subconscious. We do not have to be in hypnosis to be suggestible and pick up ideas. Sometimes a physician, baffled at a failure to cure some illness, may say to his patient, "I'm afraid you can't be helped. You'll have to learn to live with this condition." What does this mean literally? It means that the patient will die if he loses the symptom! Such an interpretation could act to prevent the patient from ever getting well or losing the symptom. He might then die. Of course the physician making such a remark did not mean it as it might be taken. With three different patients I have found this idea preventing recovery from an illness after hearing such a statement. To make such a negative suggestion is certainly unwise for it is rare that recovery is completely impossible. Even some bad cancer cases have recovered when physicians have been sure death was inevitable.

As we grow up and mature, our conscious viewpoints about many things undergo changes. The subconscious may also change its views, but more often it retains those of childhood. If something happened to you at the age of six, your subconscious is likely to continue to look at it with the viewpoint of a six-year old. A childhood incident where one is frightened by a snake may develop into a phobia about snakes which will persist, causing the person to go into a panic at seeing a harmless garter snake. Consciously it is recognized that some snakes are harmless, although repulsive. Even the picture of a snake could bring a panic reaction through this childishly retained viewpoint.

Self-punishment and guilt feelings.

Everyone exhibits compulsive behavior at times, inspired by the subconscious and often not consciously realized, unless quite illogical or unreasonable. Some of our compulsions may be quite harmful or greatly handicap us.

One of my patients, a schoolteacher, spent three or four hours daily compulsively washing her hands. They were always raw from this continual scrubbing. She could not help doing it and had no idea why it was necessary. The cause went back to something she had done with her hands for which she felt guilty. She was trying, always unsuccessfully, to wash away the guilt. Shakespeare's Lady

Macbeth washed her hands in this way, crying "Out, out, damned spot!"

Strong guilt feelings may bring a compulsion for self-punishment, which is technically called *masochism*. In large factories it has been found that 80% of the accidents happening during work occur to only 20% of the employees. This means that they are often subconsciously inspired and thus are intentional. No one wears a halo and we all do things at times for which we feel guilty. A large percentage of all accidents rise from a subconscious need for self-punishment.

This inner part of the mind seems to pay no attention to end results, but only to an immediate need. If a person compulsively has a bad accident he may lose his income for a time, may have heavy medical and hospital expense, and even be permanently crippled, or he may even be killed. If the accident was masochistic, he is not the only one being punished. His whole family will also suffer. But these end results are ignored by the subconscious. Strangely, sometimes one part of the inner mind will compel a person to do something wrong; another part, perhaps the superconscious, then punishes him for doing it.

While it may not apply to you, and would not to most smokers, undoubtedly some are using the habit self-destructively, compelled by the subconscious. Dr. Karl Menninger wrote an entire book about masochism and self-destruction (*Man Against Himself*, Harcourt Brace, New York). Many psychosomatic diseases, particularly if they are painful ones, have behind them as one of the causes a need for self-punishment which may be so strong as to be self-destructive. You may need to find out from your subconscious if masochism is involved in your smoking. I am sure this would apply only to the person who would classify as addicted to cigarettes.

How your memory works.

The subconscious is the storehouse of all your memories. Apparently we record every perception when received much as if a motion picture had been made with sound effects and with all the other senses registered, not only sight and hearing but smell, touch, and taste as well. Under hypnosis the picture can be replayed, and sometimes hypnosis is not even necessary. If you have ever tasted a lemon, just imagine you are sucking on one right now. Close your eyes and visualize the lemon, a section of it. Put it in your mouth, in your imagination. Your mouth will begin to water and you can taste the sourness. The memory brings out the actual taste.

Only a very small part of all the things that happen to us can be consciously recalled. Most of us have very few conscious memories of happenings before the age of five years. Perhaps a few very exciting or interesting events can be recalled. Now and then there may be a very early memory but often we think it is remembered when actually we have been told about it long afterwards. Nevertheless, everything that happens to us is there in our memory bank in the greatest detail. We forget consciously but the subconscious never forgets. Much that is consciously forgotten continues to affect us in various ways. Through hypnosis almost any memory can be brought back, proving the extent of unconscious memory.

In connection with smoking we have an unconscious memory working. The smoker has substituted cigarettes, cigars or a pipe for thumb-sucking which he did as a child. Even a memory of infancy is involved. As a baby you found nursing most pleasurable, and that memory is involved in your smoking habit. We all begin to smoke to feel grown-up and adult. Actually, it is thus an immaturity instead, going back to babyhood!

Very often emotional difficulties can be traced back to childhood conditioning, sometimes to traumatic (frightening or shocking) experiences. We often tend to repress the memory of unpleasant happenings. We push them out of consciousness because we don't want to think about them. Then they can't be recalled. But they may fester in the subconscious and later cause much trouble. Repressed, we then have no conscious knowledge of the cause of the trouble.

When memory begins is a good question that no one can answer for certain. Is it at a few months of age, a year, or two years, or can there be even earlier memories? Some authorities on hypnosis are convinced that there is in the subconscious an actual memory of being born. Some even believe there are real prenatal memories. Dr. Nandor Fodor wrote a book (*Search for the Beloved*, Hermitage Press, New York) trying to prove the existence of both birth and prenatal memories through the interpretations of dreams.

Under hypnosis a subject may seem to remember the experience of being born and will tell details of what seemed to have happened. However a hypnotic subject can always fantasize readily and it may not be a true memory. Personally I think such a memory may be actual, but it would be very difficult to prove it scientifically. Recalling early or repressed memories may be a great help in relieving emotional difficulties, in creating character changes, and in overcoming psychosomatic illnesses.

Your inner mind protects you.

One important duty of the inner mind is your protection. This part of the mind is always aware and functioning, whether you are awake, asleep, or unconscious. The mother of a baby may be sound asleep, but at the first whimper or cry from her child she will instantly awaken. Her subconscious has said, "Come on, wake up! Something may be wrong with the baby."

If you inadvertently touch something hot, your inner mind sends messages instantly to the muscles of your arm and you snatch your hand away long before you could think and analyze the situation. In many ways the subconscious is always alert to guard you from harm and danger. Yet, paradoxically, it may also cause illness, accidents, and even self-destruction.

Our behavioral difficulties, character disorders and traits, neuroses and psychoses, and psychosomatic illnesses are all conditions involving the subconscious part of the mind. They can be overcome by changes of both conscious and subconscious attitudes and viewpoints, changes brought about by insight into the origins and causes of these conditions.

From all that I have been saying it might seem as if there is another person inside us. Of course this is not a proper concept. We have one mind, made up of different parts. It has been compared to an iceberg floating in the ocean. The conscious part of the mind is the part of the iceberg above the water; the subconscious is the submerged part of the iceberg—a very large portion of the whole.

The total person is a unit, a mind and a body, each influencing the other. The inner mind works through the brain to control the body mechanism and to affect our behavior.

SUMMARY

This chapter should have given you a fairly good understanding of your mental make-up. You think and are aware with the conscious part of the whole mind. Below awareness is the subconscious and superconscious. Little is known about either, particularly the latter.

From automatic writing and from hypnosis we know that the subconscious part reasons, though it seems to reason rather immaturely in some ways. It takes everything literally. It often retains childhood viewpoints. It controls the entire body mechanism. It never forgets and everything that ever happens to us is in the subconscious memory, though only a small part can be consciously remembered. In hypnosis memories of forgotten experiences can be recalled. The subconscious acts to protect you from harm but sometimes it punishes for things you have done.

Unconsciously the smoker is repeating the childhood habit of thumb-sucking and is satisfying an oral craving such as was satisfied in infancy by nursing. Influencing the subconscious can be of great help in ending the smoking habit.

5

The How, Who, Where and When of Hypnosis

Many people have found that they could stop smoking without help. Some found it easy; others have had great difficulty. Many others failed. Many have been greatly helped in the quitting process by the use of hypnosis, induced either by someone else, or often through self-hypnosis. In order to have the most effective help through hypnosis, the more you know and understand about it, the better subject you are likely to be and the more it can aid you. As will be explained, it can be used also in many other ways than in ending the tobacco habit. With knowledge about it, you may wish to apply it, or have it applied, in some of these other ways, for your benefit.

In all probability you've believed many of the false ideas about hypnosis which lead people unwarrantedly to fear it. Some of these misconceptions have been mentioned. You are never unconscious while in hypnosis. You are always perfectly aware, know exactly what you're doing, and there's little sensation when you are hypnotized. Nothing clicks in your mind.

This is so true that in lighter states many subjects think they are not hypnotized when they actually are. You can always awaken yourself at any time you may wish to do so. You are not in the power of the hypnotist and can't be made to do anything contrary to your morals or that you would not ordinarily want to do. You've been spontaneously self-hypnotized many, many times, probably every day. This happens whenever you become absorbed in anything you do, and probably also whenever you're experiencing any strong emotion, such as fear, anger, or any other emotion.

All hypnosis is really auto-hypnosis, the person who may hypnotize you only being a guide. You do the work by following his suggestions and the leads he offers you. Hence it is not difficult for most people to learn to hypnotize themselves intentionally. Other chapters will tell you about self-hypnosis and how to learn it. When you have done this, it will be of the greatest advantage to you in your program of ridding yourself of the cigarette habit, and in other ways.

Hypnosis is an old art.

Hypnosis has been used since ancient times to benefit people. The priests and witch-doctors of every primitive race have employed it. In ancient Greece and Rome and Egypt and in old Oriental civilizations it was practiced. A carving in an old Egyptian temple shows a priest obviously hypnotizing a man. Primitive races today employ it. A trance was usually induced by the use of rhythm—drum beat, percussion, music, chanting, dancing, as well as by verbal suggestion. The modern use of hypnosis really began in the latter part of the eighteenth century when Anton Mesmer, a Viennese physician learned something of its applications.

The medical profession and hypnosis.

Today at least fifteen thousand physicians, dentists, and psychologists have had instruction in the applications of hypnosis. There are such men in every large city, in most smaller ones, and even in many small towns. There are three national professional societies made up of these men, with a total of several thousand members.

It is impossible to say how many patients have benefitted from being hypnotized. Many thousands of women have gone through childbirth while in hypnosis, for scores of obstetricians have learned to employ it. Some of the leaders in this field have delivered personally over a thousand women in this way.

In Los Angeles there is a "hypnodontic" society numbering some 150 dentists as members, and there are chapters of the national societies in many cities. This will give you some idea of the extensive use being made of hypnosis today in this country. There are also hypnotic societies in many other countries.

Ever since the days of Mesmer until recently the medical profession has frowned on those of its members who have dared employ hypnosis, and tended to ostracize them. However, many found it so valuable in their work that they continued to use it in spite of the attitude of their colleagues. Today the situation is quite different.

A few years ago the British Medical Association set up a committee to investigate the medical applications of hypnosis. It reported most favorably, after studying the matter for some time, and the association then accepted the report and recommended that physicians learn its techniques—that it be taught in the medical schools.

In 1958 our American Medical Association appointed a similar committee and its report was like that of the British. Our A.M.A. then approved the use of hypnosis by its members. Being conservative, only a very few medical schools have yet begun to teach hypnosis to medical students or in postgraduate courses. The same applies to the dental schools, although more of them have given such courses. Most professional men have learned in privately given classes, such as are offered by *Hypnosis Symposiums,* a group with which I am one of the instructors. We have given these courses—some eighty of them—in many cities and in Canada, Mexico, and the Caribbean. Other similar groups have also offered such instruction, open only to professional men. All of this shows that hypnosis is now acceptable in medicine, dentistry and psychology, and is being found by its practitioners as of great benefit to their patients.

Hypnosis on the stage and television.

One of the things leading many people to be afraid of hypnosis has come from watching stage or television shows. Usually the stage hypnotist apparently makes hypnotized subjects do ridiculous things. Why will those who act as subjects for these performers make such fools of themselves? With experience, the stage hypnotist has learned to be able to pick his subjects carefully. He uses only those whom he knows will be able to become deeply hypnotized. In TV performances a trained subject is always used, though the hypnotist may pretend the subject has never been hypnotized and is a stranger to him.

Many who go up on the stage to be hypnotized are exhibitionists. They have a good time and do not mind doing foolish things, with the excuse that they are hypnotized and must do them. Others have the idea that they are in the hypnotist's power and must do anything they are told to do. If it is not too obnoxious, it will be done. But if a stage hypnotist told a woman subject to remove her clothes, she would either awaken herself indignantly, or simply refuse to do it. Such subjects will not do anything too drastic. The stage operator knows this and does not suggest anything too objectionable.

In almost every country in the world except the English-speaking ones public demonstrations are barred by law. A few states in this country are passing such laws and restricting the use of hypnosis to properly qualified professional men. Such laws are badly needed, for hypnosis lends itself too readily to quackery.

In many cities the classified columns in the newspapers carry advertisements of treatment by these unqualified men, offering to "cure" anything from warts to the worst neurotic conditions. The sensible person will beware and stay out of the clutches of anyone so advertising. Ethical practitioners never advertise.

While dangers are slight in qualified hands, there are some when uninformed people "monkey" with hypnosis, out of curiosity. While bad results are rare even with unqualified hypnotists, they could occur. It is foolish to let such a person hypnotize you.

Is hypnosis dangerous?

Some psychiatrists have reached the conclusion that hypnosis when practiced by non-psychiatrists is quite dangerous. From them have come various articles in both popular magazines and in medical journals, stressing the dangers. Usually these authors are quite unknown in hypnotic professional circles. The mere fact of being a psychiatrist is no indication of having any knowledge of hypnosis or of being an authority about it. As a definite fact most psychiatrists know nothing about it and have had no training in hypnotic techniques. Most have never seen anyone hypnotized, for few medical schools teach it, even in psychiatric training.

For you to appreciate the real dangers, and realize that they are really very few, some of the claims as to these dangers should be cited. The most often mentioned one is that a person who is greatly disturbed or on the verge of a psychosis (insanity) may become psychotic if he is hypnotized. There is some truth in this but not the way it is mentioned. Undoubtedly an extremely disturbed or greatly depressed person should not be hypnotized, unless perhaps by a psychiatrist who would know how to handle the hypnosis. Such a person should not use self-hypnosis. This is definitely a contraindication, and the only one.

Merely being hypnotized never caused anyone to "go off his rocker." No one ever became psychotic just because he was hypnotized. Dr. Milton Erickson, a psychiatrist and one of the leading authorities on hypnosis, has stated this as true, but that hypnosis might be misused by the operator with such a result. It would not be hypnosis itself but its misuse which caused this. Since you would hardly misuse it on yourself, you can dismiss this idea as to it being dangerous for you to hypnotize yourself. Actually, there have been very few cases reported of anyone going insane while undergoing hypnotic treatment, though it has happened. It has also happened many times with any other form of treatment.

Another criticism of the use of hypnosis has been in reference to the removal of some symptom or condition by suggestion. Hypnotherapy usually includes applying hypnosis to uncover the causes of any condition or symptom, but sometimes they can be removed by suggestion.

One of the cases where a bad result supposedly developed was that of a blind woman. Her blindness was emotionally caused, and was not physical. She did not want to see for some reason and so lost her vision. Hypnotic suggestion was used to bring recovery and her sight returned. Soon afterwards she stabbed her lover. It was claimed that loss of her symptom of blindness caused her to do this. Of course she may have wanted to stab him long before but could not because of her blindness. And who knows what quarrel there was just before her act. Loss of her symptom and hypnosis may have had nothing to do with it.

Another such case cited was that of a very obese woman who was treated with hypnotic suggestion and lost many pounds. When she had slimmed down, she committed suicide. Her act was blamed on removal of her symptom of overweight. Actually, her suicide may have had nothing to do with loss of her symptom. No one knows her motives for self-destruction. In most of the cases where bad results have been claimed to follow the use of hypnosis, the critics have leaped at the conclusion that hypnosis caused the bad effect, where it may not have been involved at all.

It should be mentioned that there are lots of psychiatrists who have had much experience with hypnosis who do not accept these criticisms as justified. They do not think hypnosis extremely dangerous, though of course it can be misused. A qualified therapist knows how to avoid the possible dangers. It should be emphasized that no bad results have ever been reported from the use of self-hypnosis. Its freedom from danger is apparent when you realize that we all are so frequently spontaneously self-hypnotized.

One slight danger should be mentioned as applying to both hetero- or auto-hypnosis. When some hypnotic phenomenon is induced, it should always be ended, or a time set for it to end. For example, if hypnotic anesthesia is induced it should have an ending set. Pain has a meaning and is nature's warning of something wrong. A pain in the abdomen might be an indication of appendicitis. If hypnotic anesthesia were induced the appendix might burst without the person being aware of it. No pain should be shut off in this way without knowing what is causing it. Chronic headaches might be controlled by suggestion, but if they were resulting from a brain tumor it would be folly to suppress a headache. Any suggestion not intended to act posthypnotically should be removed, as should any phenomena that were induced.

Who can be hypnotized?

Possibly you wonder if you can be hypnotized. Almost everyone has the impression that he will not be a very good subject. Often, when patients come to me, they will remark, "I don't think I'll be a good subject. I have too strong a mind." Then they promptly go into a good depth of trance when induction is made.

In fact, the stronger and better your mind, the more likely you are to be a good subject. People with little intelligence, or the "flighty" type are often hard to hypnotize. They can't concentrate well or follow the suggestions

given them. The better your I.Q., the more apt you are
to be a good subject. However, many other things enter
the picture and it might be impossible to hypnotize a
genius or, on the other hand, a stupid person sometimes
makes a good subject.

Probably everyone is potentially a deep trance subject.
Fears, doubts, and other matters can enter to hold one
back when hypnosis is attempted. The skill of the operator
and his choice of method would also be involved.

Children make the very best subjects, usually able to
be deeply hypnotized. They are very suggestible or they
could not learn readily, this making them more hypnotiza-
ble. If we were to make a graph of hypnotizability it
would be a sharply ascending line with a peak at the ages
of six to eight years, then a very gradually descending
line with additional age.

As a rule elderly people are harder to hypnotize, probably because of being more rigid and set in their ways.
Those in their teens and twenties are usually good subjects. However, at any age it all depends on the individual
and some old folks are very good subjects. One of the
best with whom I've worked was an eighty-four year old
woman. Still others of the elderly have been good subjects. Conversely, a few children will resist and can't be
hypnotized, though they usually cooperate and find it interesting and fun to be hypnotized. As a matter of fact, no
one can be hypnotized unless he is willing and cooperative.

To give some statistics, nineteen out of twenty people
can be hypnotized at least lightly, and for most purposes
a light state is quite sufficient. If we had to depend on
deep hypnosis for results it would not be very practical.
Only about one in eight or ten learns to become deeply

hypnotized—to reach what is called a somnambulistic state.

Here is a table showing some statistics:
5% of people are unhypnotizable,
35% will become lightly hypnotized,
45% can reach a medium depth,
15% will enter a deep trance.

These figures are for an average population. It would be entirely different for children, different in the other direction for old folks.

There seems to be little or no difference between the sexes, though in my experience women do not seem to have as many fears about being hypnotized. Perhaps they are a bit more curious than are the males! Race or physical characteristics do not seem to make any difference. Provided a person has first been hypnotized by someone else, these figures would apply to self-hypnosis as well as where an operator induces it. Otherwise the percentages would be smaller as to self-hypnosis. From these statistics you will see that most readers of this book will be able to hypnotize themselves, using the methods to be given later.

SUMMARY

Hypnosis has been known and used throughout history. In modern times it has been opposed until very recently by the medical profession but from investigation into its possibilities our A.M.A. now advises its members to learn and use it.

Professional men frown on stage and TV performances with hypnosis, and urge passing of laws forbidding such use and to prevent quacks and charlatans from using hypnosis. You will have seen that dangers in employing hypnosis are minimal, despite some criticism from a few psychiatrists who apparently know little about hypnosis. No one has ever gone insane because of being hypnotized, although there have been such results from its misuse, just as there are with any other form of treatment. Symptom removal by suggestion has been termed dangerous, but there is no proof that this is so. No bad result has ever been reported in the use of self-hypnosis.

Only about one person out of twenty cannot be hypnotized. Children make the best subjects, elderly people being more difficult, although some will be found to be good subjects. In general, the greater the person's intelligence, the more likely he is to be a good subject. There seems to be no difference in hypnotizability between males and females.

6

How Hypnosis Has Helped Others

You should know something of how hypnosis is used and the phenomena which can be produced by a hypnotized person.

Pain can be shut off: hypnotic anesthesia.

Wouldn't it be good to be able to shut off pain at any time it developed? Of course it should only be done under the proper conditions, but if you hurt yourself in some way, being able to stop the pain would certainly be a blessing. A good hypnotic subject can usually learn to do this. Pain can be modified greatly and sometimes controlled completely even if you are only in a medium state of hypnosis. Sometimes it is possible to control it where hypnosis is only light.

Depth of hypnosis is termed as light, medium, or deep, although there is a still deeper stage which is very seldom produced, for it takes a very good subject to experience it with several hours of continued induction. It has no very practical purpose that isn't found in lighter stages. This has been called a plenary trance.

Hypnotic anesthesia can be so complete that many major surgical operations have been carried out with it and with no drugs used at all. Limbs have been amputated, the chest opened and heart surgery performed, a lung removed, and many other serious types of operation carried out with the patient free of pain. Such procedure is not usual, of course, for it is easier to use drug anesthetics. But sometimes drugs cannot be used for some reason and then hypnotic anesthesia is very valuable.

Before anesthetic drugs were discovered, surgery was a terrible ordeal for the patient, who was conscious throughout unless pain became so great that he fainted. In the eighteen-forties, a British surgeon in India experimented with hypnosis for surgery and performed over three thousand operations, including more than three hundred classed as major, using only hypnosis. His name was James Esdaile. Soon afterwards it was found how chloroform and ether could make a person unconscious, and hypnotic anesthesia was never utilized to any extent again until recently. Of course it is not often used now except for childbirth and when drugs can't be used.

To understand how hypnotic anesthesia works, the usually accepted theory of pain should be explained. Understanding this will make it easier for you to produce hypnotic anesthesia in yourself when you might wish to do so. Pain nerves work on a tiny electric impulse. Pain may be stimulated in your hand, for instance, but the impulse must be carried along the nerve channels and must register in your brain or you do not feel pain. In theory, local anesthetic drugs act to block or paralyze the nerves so the impulse doesn't reach the brain. All you feel then is a numbness in the area, such as the jaw if a dentist injects novocaine there.

How self-hypnosis saved a life.

Did you ever find you were bleeding and on investigating discover you had cut yourself, perhaps rather badly? Until you located the cut you may have felt no pain. Then it began to hurt. Soldiers in the excitement of battle sometimes are badly wounded and yet do not feel pain for some time.

One of my patients was a paraplegic who had lost both hands during a Korean battle. A shell had exploded killing all the members of his squad. A fragment had blown off both his hands. He was stunned but quickly revived and saw the blood pouring from one of his wrists. He knew he must shut it off and reached with the other arm to do so, but then saw that that hand was also gone, that wrist also bleeding badly.

This man had learned self-hypnosis and was a very good subject. He realized he would soon bleed to death. Quickly hypnotizing himself he told himself the blood vessels would contract until the blood escaping from the wounds stopped flowing and coagulated. He also suggested he would feel no pain from the wounds. Within a few moments the blood had stopped flowing and had clotted. He lay on the ground for almost two hours before being picked up and taken to a hospital. He said he felt that he could not die because of having three small children dependent on him. This motivation, together with his own will to live, undoubtedly saved his life.

Hypnotic age regression.

Everything that has ever happened to us as our lives
are lived seems to be registered in our memory. We can
only draw consciously on a very small part of these memories, only an infinitesimal bit, when we consider all the
minute details of our experiences. Under hypnosis most
of these memories can be recovered. A subject can be
caused to relive experiences, this being termed age regression. Even very early experiences in our lives can be recalled in this way.

Perhaps we can even be age regressed to the time when
we were born. It is very difficult to prove scientifically
that anyone has such a thing in the subconscious mind as
an actual memory of birth. However many hypnotic practitioners think such a memory may be present and is real.
Of course any subject can fantasize readily and sometimes
it is hard to know if a supposed memory is real or only a
fantasy.

The patient of one psychiatrist brought out when regressed that she had been born by caesarian section,
claiming after awakening that she had not known of this.
Her mother confirmed it, but it is always a possibility that
she had been told of this by her mother or had heard it
mentioned at some time and then had forgotten it. It
may not have been a true memory. It is this that makes
scientific proof of the actuality of birth memories so difficult.

There are two forms of age regression. One might be
called complete regression, though of course it is never
really complete. With this type, if a person is told he is
five years old, he behaves as would one at that age and

seems to know nothing of the time from then to the present. If regressed to a year old or other time in infancy, he would not be able to talk and would drool and coo as would any baby, perhaps crying as a baby cries. He will even show physical reflexes such as are present in infancy but which are lost with growth. This type of regression requires a very deep state of hypnosis for its production.

The other type of regression is easily induced in just a light state of hypnosis. It could be called a partial regression. When you've learned self-hypnosis you can even do it readily yourself. There's a kind of duality in it. You relive some past happening just as it originally took place, with all five of your senses working as you relive it. You see, you hear, feel, and if taste and smell were involved, you have those perceptions. If taken back to a time when you were hurt, you even feel pain, just as you originally did, but without as much intensity.

At the same time while you are thus regressed, you are well aware of your actual environment. You tell of what is happening and can speak even if the regression was to infancy when you did not know language.

This type of regression frequently is useful in hypnotherapy. Often things that happen to us in childhood continue to affect us in later life, although consciously we may not even remember the experience. Often it is necessary in psychotherapy to take a person back and let him see how such a happening has influenced him or is perhaps one of the causes for some psychosomatic illness or symptom. With insight, its effect can be removed.

This is one of the great advantages in hypnotherapy as compared with more orthodox therapy. Often a condition, even a neurosis, can be cleared up in only a few sessions when it would require many, many hours with the usual psychoanalysis or psychiatry. Hypnotherapy offers a great shortcut. Age regression is one of its most valuable techniques.

Penfield, a Canadian physician has found that age regression can be produced by electrical stimulation of the brain lobes. This seems to produce the same effect as is brought about by suggestion of age regression.

Age regression has even been used to advantage in police work, an application mostly overlooked. In Los Angeles, two bandits held up a jewelry store. As the men ran out and made their getaway in a car, a young couple were passing by. They were questioned by the police but could not remember having noticed the license number of the car. They were then separately hypnotized and regressed to the incident. Both then told of watching the men get into the car and drive away, and both gave the license plate numbers. Subconsciously they had registered the numbers but were consciously unaware of having done so. The holdup men were traced through the license and arrested.

Another practical application of age regression is in finding lost or mislaid articles. This has often been accomplished. Of course the subconscious mind must know what has been done with the lost article or it could not bring out the knowledge.

Most physicians who have little or no knowledge of hypnosis are not aware that the subconscious part of the mind is always alert and aware. Even when the conscious part is drugged as with anesthesia, or when there is any period of unconsciousness such as from a blow or in sleep, the inner mind still hears and registers. With age regression a subject can be returned to an operation and can then tell all that happened while he was in the deepest stage of anesthesia. Surgeons and anesthesiologists who have become aware of this now give beneficial suggestions to patients while they are "out." In this way, post-operative shock and nausea can be prevented. Rapid healing can be promoted, and urine retention prevented, this last often being a complication following surgery.

How time can be distorted.

Most hypnotic phenomena was known within a few years after the days of Mesmer. In 1823 a tooth was extracted with hypnotic anesthesia and not long after a woman was hypnotized for childbirth. Some ten years ago the late Dr. Lynn Cooper, of Washington, D.C., made a discovery of a previously unknown phenomenon, which he called time distortion.

It's been reported at times that a drowning person has recalled long periods of his life during only two or three moments while drowning. Dreams which seem to occupy a long period of time may only last a moment or so.

This speeding up of thought can be produced by hypnotic suggestion. Cooper made tests of this. One was to give a hypnotized person a mathematical problem to solve which would ordinarily take about ten minutes to work out. He would be told to listen to a metronome set to beat once a minute and was to solve the problem by the tenth beat. However, the metronome actually beat once a second and in ten seconds the answer would be reached. Many other different kinds of tests of this ability were also made. It requires a good depth of trance.

Dr. Raymond LaScola, who has written the foreword of this book, is a concert pianist as well as a physician. Busy with his medical work, he is often unable to practice piano as much as he wishes. By hypnotizing himself and using time distortion, he practices mentally for a few moments, getting all the benefit he would from several hours of actual practice.

A subject can hallucinate.

When deeply hypnotized any subject is able to hallucinate readily and some types of hallucinations can even be produced in a medium state. Any of the five senses can be hallucinated by suggestion to that effect. The subject can be told he sees something that isn't present, or doesn't see something that is there—a positive or a negative hallucination.

Sometimes both types can be provoked at the same time. The subject can be told a person sitting in a chair near him has left the room. Instructed to open his eyes, he has a negative hallucination for the person actually sitting in the chair and does not see him. At the same time, he does see the chair which is really hidden by the body of the person sitting in it, which is a positive hallucination.

Some hallucinations, such as of taste or smell can even be invoked when a subject is only in a medium state of hypnosis. The senses of hearing and sight seem to require a deep stage. In self-hypnosis it would be better not to attempt to produce any kind of hallucination, just in case it might carry over into the waking state. Such hallucinations are best let alone, though probably this would be harmless.

Catalepsy—another interesting phenomenon.

When you are hypnotized, even lightly, a change in the tone of your muscles seems to take place. This has been called catalepsy. By definition, it is a change in muscular tonus which may be either extreme rigidity or it may be the opposite, great flaccidity. When flaccid, if an arm is lifted, it feels as if there was no bone in it, kind of rubbery. Another aspect of catalepsy is the tendency of a limb to stay in any position in which it's placed, even an uncomfortable one. Left there for some time, it doesn't even feel tired.

In a deeper stage the entire body may be caused to become cataleptic if this is suggested (made rigid). Stage hypnotists often do this in their performances. The subject is told he is becoming stiff and rigid, that he will be as stiff as a board. With repetition of these suggestions he does become rigid. The operator will then lay him across two chairs, his head on one, his feet on the other. Probably he will then seat himself or stand on the subject's stomach. Of course there is danger in this. The subject might have a weak back or this might cause a hernia. Strangely, with such catalepsy the person need make no great effort to hold himself rigid and can support much weight without caving in. It is such performances that disgust professional men who use hypnosis and lead them to urge legislation forbidding public demonstrations.

SUMMARY

You have now learned some of the very interesting phenomena which a subject can experience—anesthesia, age regression, hallucinations, time distortion, and catalepsy. You will realize that there are some possible dangers if hypnosis is misused, but they are minimal and seldom do such cases arise. You know also that self-hypnosis is free from danger.

Historically, hypnosis has lacked acceptance by the medical profession, due to lack of proper information about it, though this attitude has recently changed completely. Now for the first time hypnosis is seen and medically accepted as a legitimate procedure.

7

Learning How to Recognize and Use Hypnosis

We know a good deal about hypnosis and its phenomena, but just what is it? We also know much about how to use electricity but we don't know what it is, and no one really knows what hypnosis is. We can describe it but no entirely correct theory has ever been devised about it that fits in every way. It's a state of altered awareness with much of a hypnotized person's thinking rising directly from the subconscious. It's a state of greatly increased suggestibility, marked by great relaxation.

Describing hypnosis doesn't give us a theory about it. A difficulty in this is that a light state of hypnosis is very different from a deep somnambulistic state. When you are in a deep state there is a definite awareness that things are different. We could make a comparison. Think of a teeter-totter. In the waking state the conscious part of the mind is at the upper end, the subconscious at the lower end. As you drift into hypnosis the upper end goes down, with the subconscious part rising nearer the surface. This means we have better access to it and can influence it easier. The conscious part remains aware though at the low end of the teeter-totter.

The signs or symptoms of hypnosis.

When hypnotizing someone, the operator watches his subject closely, observing what is happening and looking for certain signs or symptoms. There is often a rather normal apprehension felt by a subject the first time he's hypnotized. Almost anyone will feel this during any new experience. As soon as he becomes well relaxed he finds himself very comfortable and any apprehension fades away. A faster pulse and more rapid breathing are signs of anxiety and the operator watches for this. The pulse in the subject's neck is usually visible and can be seen to throb. When apprehension is lost the heartbeat and breathing rate both slow down to a little less than they were in the waking state. Probably this is only a matter of greater relaxation.

As a person drifts into hypnosis, when his eyes have closed it is quite usual for the lids to begin to flutter. This is only a sign of a light state and is not always present. With a little more depth reached, the flutter usually stops. If not, the operator would suggest more relaxation of the eyelid muscles and then the fluttering stops. Observing this fluttering of the eyelids tells the operator his subject is in a light state.

A hypnotized person can move if he wishes, but the lethargy is usually great enough so this seems to be too much trouble. Every few moments while you are sitting in a chair or lying down you will invariably move and shift your position a bit. While in hypnosis a person seldom moves at all, even if left in the state for two or three hours or even longer. I've seen a fly light on a subject's face and stroll around. In a light stage of hypnosis it would be quickly brushed off; but even if the depth is only medium it is unlikely to be shooed away. Asked after awakening if he felt the fly on his face, the subject will say, "Oh, yes. I knew it was there but it didn't seem to matter. It was too much trouble to brush it off."

Even in light hypnosis relaxation seems to smooth out the lines of the face. Soon there is a complete lack of expression. This is very noticeable. If the subject's eyes are opened there is a glassy appearance, a stare. With the eyes closed, the eyeballs can often be seen to have rolled up, as though looking up at the forehead. When this happens, the lids may be partly open with the whites of the eyes showing at the bottom. This would be an indication of at least a medium trance depth.

As there's so little sensation when you are hypnotized, the operator may suggest some test or some phenomena so you'll have more realization of being hypnotized—that something is different. He may suggest that you can't open your eyes and when you try you find they won't open. He may tell you one arm is becoming so heavy that you can't lift it, and you find you do not have enough strength to raise it. He may ask you to clasp your hands together, lacing the fingers. With a suggestion that you can't take them apart, you struggle but they stay locked together.

Another way of helping the subject realize he is hypnotized is to induce some phenomenon, such as anesthesia, perhaps in one hand. When he feels little or no pain when it is stimulated he realizes he is in hypnosis.

Another test which might be made is to suggest that all the weight of one arm is being lost, that it will begin to feel lighter and lighter until it begins to bend at the elbow and the hand floats up towards the subject's face. With repeated suggestions it slowly lifts of its own accord, without any voluntary effort needed.

Frequently when a subject is awakened, he will rub his eyes, much as we tend to do when we awaken from sleep. Sometimes the subject's mouth twitches a little and he may give a slight start as he awakens.

Does a subject have amnesia after awakening?

In stage or TV demonstrations, when a person is awakened he may seem to have no memory of what has just occurred while he was hypnotized—an amnesia for the entire experience. Such an amnesia is sometimes spontaneous, but it never happens unless the person has been in a very deep state and it is even rare then. Demonstration subjects are always carefully selected as being capable of a deep trance, and the amnesia shown afterwards is usually suggested by the operator.

Amnesia can be induced by suggestion or it can be prevented. It may be complete or only partial. Complete amnesia is only seen if the subject has been in a deep state. A partial amnesia can often be developed when there is only a medium depth. In this case the subject is told to forget some particular thing that he has done while hypnotized, or some particular suggestion which has been given him. I've never heard of a person using self-hypnosis developing amnesia after awakening.

Finding the depth of hypnosis.

The experienced operator observes his subject closely as hypnosis is induced, and continues this until the person is awakened. Through observation he is able to sense or estimate how deeply the subject goes into hypnosis.

When you are using self-hypnosis you will want to know how deeply you go. Your own subconscious mind can give this information. It must have a yardstick with which to measure. This can be just an imaginary yardstick, of thirty-six inches. We can say that a light state of hypnosis is the first foot—one to twelve inches. A medium state is twelve to twenty-four inches and a deep state is twenty-four to thirty-six inches on our yardstick.

While you are still hypnotized, imagine this yardstick standing on end in front of you, close to you. The one inch end is at the top. In your imagination see a white arrow or indicator pointing at the one inch mark. Now you suggest to yourself that the indicator is going to slide down the yardstick and stop at the inch mark registering the greatest depth you have reached. Usually you will see it slide down and stop someplace. You then read the number and this will tell you the depth. Actual testing indicates that the answer is almost always a valid one.

Using hypnosis—controlling bodily processes.

It can readily be shown how hypnotic suggestion can cause the subconscious mind to control or change some of the physical mechanisms of the body. Some research, but not any great amount, has been carried out along these lines. It is quite possible that the inner mind regulates all the body mechanisms.

It has been mentioned that healing can be speeded up and blood circulation affected. Heart beat can be speeded up or slowed down by suggestion; the body temperature raised or lowered somewhat. If told the room is very cold, a subject may actually produce gooseflesh, as well as shiver and say he feels cold. Metabolism can be affected and digestive processes changed, but we don't know too much about what action of other organs and glands can be affected. Chronic constipation usually can be ended readily. In some illnesses there can be much benefit from such controls.

Hypnosis can be of great value in psychotherapy and much can be accomplished with self-hypnosis. Character traits, habits, many minor neurotic difficulties (if not too deep-seated) can be changed or overcome with self-hypnosis and proper methods. There is no better way to overcome insomnia, to eliminate excess weight, and to remedy many psychosomatic illnesses than through hypnosis. I have gone into detail on self-treatment of these conditions in my book, *Self-Hypnotism, The Technique and Its Use in Daily Living* (Prentice-Hall, Englewood Cliffs, N.J.)

Using self-hypnosis for learning.

People often complain of having difficulty concentrating and hence don't learn readily. I've helped several college students and others with this problem. Taught self-hypnosis, if one can learn to open his eyes while staying in hypnosis, he is able to shut out distractions, to concentrate far better. Then there is better registration of what is being studied and recall is far better.

It is possible to take an examination while in hypnosis and remembering is much easier. If you've learned self-hypnosis and ever have occasion to study anything, or if you have trouble concentrating, you'll find it of great advantage for this purpose. Sometimes lack of concentration has some psychological reason behind it. There may be some subconscious reason why you have trouble keeping your attention focused. It might be that the causes would need to be uncovered and understood so that any such block could be removed.

Overcoming that tired feeling.

When we become tired, chemical changes take place in the body tissues. This may be gradual or very rapid if we exert greatly. A day's work may bring fatigue; an athlete might develop it in only a moment or so with extreme exertion.

Strangely, the inner mind seems to be able to inhibit or prevent fatigue to a large extent—the chemical changes don't take place. If you are already fatigued, it can bring the tissue chemistry back to normal in a short time and the tiredness is gone.

Years ago the old time stage hypnotists often made use of this ability of the subconscious mind to affect the body and prevent fatigue. The hypnotist often travelled around the country giving one night shows in each town. He would have a highly trained, excellent hypnotic subject employed who had been taught self-hypnosis and how to inhibit fatigue. This might be a young man or sometimes a girl.

By prearrangement this subject would go to the town where the hypnotist was to appear the next day. If it was a man, he would enter a store window and mount a bicycle with its rear wheel jacked up. Self-hypnotized and with the suggestion of no fatigue, he would peddle rapidly for about twenty-four hours without stopping, even to go to the bathroom. If it was a girl, she would seat herself at a piano and play continuously for about that length of time without stopping.

There may be times when you are quite tired and you will find you can lose most of the fatigued feeling by hypnotizing yourself and giving yourself suggestions to end the feeling.

It's not a panacea.

It should be remembered that hypnosis is not able to work miracles and is not a magic wand. It merely offers a means of influencing the subconscious mind and through it can perhaps affect bodily processes. Individuals vary greatly in their reactions. Suggestions are not always effective and we don't have the desired result. We are dealing with something intangible. Also we simply do not know enough about the mind, particularly about the subconscious part.

SUMMARY

We know much about hypnosis, but not what it really is. You know now some of the signs a subject shows as he enters hypnosis or while hypnotized, fluttering of the eyelids, respiration and pulse changes, etc. Amnesia can be suggested to a subject, or it can be prevented from occurring.

You can learn the depth of hypnosis you reach by having your subconscious measure it on an imaginary yardstick. The inner mind can control bodily activities and can overcome feelings of fatigue. Another useful application of hypnosis is in learning—better concentration and recall. Although much can be done through hypnosis and suggestion, it is not a magic wand and there are failures.

8

How to Use
Auto-Suggestion

Suggestion is one of the best ways of influencing the subconscious mind. In general, that part of the mental makeup tends to be uncritical. Suggestion has been defined as the uncritical acceptance of an idea.

We are all suggestible in varying degree and especially so during childhood. If you were not suggestible it would be difficult to learn, which is why children are so suggestible. They are at a stage where they need to learn rapidly. When we are under hypnosis we become extremely suggestible and this is also true when we are under any emotion. Sometimes suggestibility is mistakenly confused with gullibility. Gullibility is the quality of being easily fooled. Being suggestible is an asset, but being gullible is a liability.

You'll be using suggestion as one of the factors which will help you in your program of ending the tobacco habit. So it can be used most effectively, it is important to know the laws which govern suggestion. Hetero-suggestion (that given by someone else) is more powerful than self-suggestion, but the latter can be quite effective, particularly with knowledge of how best to apply it. Suggestibility is increased considerably when you are in even a light state of hypnosis. Auto-hypnosis and auto-suggestion will help you greatly in making the process of stopping smoking relatively easy.

Types of suggestions.

We can classify suggestions as being either commanding or permissive in the way they are given. They may be direct or indirect; positive or negative in nature. Auto-suggestions are usually direct rather than indirect, but they can be given in a permissive way or commandingly. A positive suggestion has much more force than a negative one. To make a suggestion positive, you should avoid such words as "not," "don't," "won't," and "can't." "I'll not want to smoke any more" is a negative suggestion. "I'll be free of all desire to smoke" is a positive one.

A permissive suggestion is more likely to be acceptable to the subconscious mind and to be carried out than is a dominating command. Most everyone resents being ordered to do something. With auto-suggestion, your inner mind may resent a command and will be more cooperative as a rule if asked to do something rather than ordered to do it.

Sometimes, and with some individuals, commands may be best. People react differently. There may be an unconscious need to be dominated. Then commands would be best. In phrasing suggestions the words "you can" are permissive. "You will" is a command. A suggestion may be given forcefully and still be permissive. The words used might seem to be permissive and yet the suggestor's attitude, manner, and tone of voice might be dominating.

How to make suggestions most effective.

Repetition is the most important rule to follow in making suggestions work best. They should be repeated three or four times, or even more often. All advertising is based on suggestion and advertising attempts to influence the subconscious part of the mind rather than the consciousness. All advertisers know that the effect of repeated ads is cumulative. Television commercials are repeated again and again, to the point of nausea, as you have undoubtedly noticed. Some commercials are nothing but the old carnival pitchman patter of the most obnoxious type. Yet these commercials are effective in causing people to buy the advertised products. A few people are driven away but more succumb and buy. (As a side observation, results from TV commercials would be far greater if advertisers knew more of the principles and laws of suggestion and hypnosis.)

In giving suggestions it is important to allow enough time for a suggestion to be accepted by the subconscious and then carried out. It should be worded so the effect is for the immediate future rather than the present. If you have the urge to smoke during your quitting program and try to overcome the desire, it would be futile to say, "I don't want to smoke." It is contrary to fact. It is a negative suggestion, and the idea could not be accepted instantly. If worded, "In a moment the desire to smoke will dwindle away and I'll forget about it" it is positive and is put into the immediate future. It allows time for the idea to be assimilated and carried out.

In giving auto-suggestion it isn't necessary to say the words aloud. You can merely think them. Some people do respond better if the words are spoken, so you might experiment as to this in your own case.

If there is some motivation for the acceptance of a suggestion the more likely it is to be carried out. The more motivation you have to stop smoking, the easier it will be to quit. In giving you a program to follow, all possible motivations will be stressed. Arousing an emotion and attaching it to a suggestion will make it more effective. This could be through words or a visual image or both. Desire for success could be one motive aroused, with shame over possible failure.

Using visual imagery.

If a visual image can be formed and attached to a verbal suggestion, it makes the suggestion more powerful. There is a tendency on the part of the subconscious to carry out any prolonged and repeated visual image. It is not always possible to think of a suitable one to accompany a particular suggestion.

In my practice I'm sometimes asked to help an actor or actress overcome stage fright. When the late Marilyn Monroe was first attempting to become a motion picture actress she had an extreme case of stage fright. With several good opportunities she lost out because she would be paralyzed and speechless when the cameras started to film. Marilyn overcame this by the use of hypnosis and suggestion, one of the techniques being to have her, while self-hypnotized, imagine herself going through a scene, seeing herself composed and at ease, moving about and speaking to other imagined actors.

As another example, in treating obesity with a woman patient, I ask her to get a photograph of herself, if possible, when she was slender. If she doesn't have one, she is asked to cut a picture from a magazine of a girl in a bathing suit whose figure is as she would like her own to be. She is to take the head from a picture of herself, paste it on this magazine picture and fasten the composite picture to her mirror. Every time she looks in the mirror she is to look at the picture and think of it as being herself. Then in bed at night she is to shut her eyes and visualize herself as she would like to be, as in the picture.

You will apply this idea in your program of ending the tobacco habit. You could visualize yourself in a smoke-filled room with a number of other people, all smoking but yourself. See yourself coughing, disgusted with the choking atmosphere. Add anything else unpleasant about such a scene that you can think of.

Other helpful rules about suggestion.

Don't burden your subconscious with too many suggestions at one time. It is better to work on only one thing at a time, or at most two. Otherwise the effect is diffused. Work with repetition on one or two suggestions for two or three sessions, then go to others. After repeating these in the same way, return to the first ones.

Word suggestions with only the end result in mind. Be specific as to your goal. Your inner mind knows far better than your conscious mind how to reach the goal. Stimulate it into action and it will find the means. Applying this to your stopping smoking program, the one suggestion, "I will soon be rid of the desire to smoke" covers everything. If you have no desire, you'll not smoke.

Acceptance by the inner mind is needed for any suggestion to be carried out, no matter how much you consciously may want it to be effective. When a permissive suggestion has been repeated but without result, it would be a good thing to try rewording it as a command instead.

Some writers have made quite a point as to the wording of suggestions in the use of *I* or *you*—first person or second for auto-suggestion. You might experiment as to this, but I believe the subconscious mind will accept either form as applying to you. This seems to be proved by the fact that, in therapy, suggestions which have been carried out are found to be worded either way or both ways.

Suggestions can be either helpful to us or harmful. They can work in both directions. We are constantly bombarded with suggestions, many of them negative. An unpleasant trick has been played sometimes on some individual in an office. He arrives in the morning and a fellow worker greets him with the remark, "Good heavens, Jim, you must have had a bad night. You look terrible this morning. Did you hang one on?" Jim has been feeling quite well and is surprised at these remarks. A little later someone casually remarks, "Got a hangover this morning, Jim? You sure look bad." Another inquires sympathetically if perhaps Jim has a fever. By this time Jim feels poorly and further repetition is likely to send him home actually ill.

How suggestion affects medical research.

When medical research is carried on to find the effect of some drug, the power of suggestion and the degree of suggestibility found in most people is always a consideration. In research it is always necessary to use what is called a "control" group of subjects. A number of people in one group are given the drug being tested. Another group is given a placebo—something that looks like the real drug but which is inert. A sugar pill may be used as the placebo.

The effect on both groups is studied. It is found that a large percentage of the control group responds to the placebo just as do those subjects who have taken the real drug. This is due to suggestion. These subjects thought they had taken the real drug and reacted accordingly. In fact, the effect of suggestion has been so great that it has been found necessary to keep those administering the drug in the dark as to which persons receive the drug and which get the placebo. Otherwise, subjects manage to pick up clues from the person doing the testing. This has been called "double blind" testing.

Other techniques to practice.

Max Freedom Long has made quite a study of suggestion and how best to make it effective. In his book, *Self-Suggestion* (Huna Research Publications, Vista, Calif.) he stresses the use of deep breathing while giving oneself suggestions. Long says to breathe deeply and hard, at the same time concentrating intently on the suggestion and "pulsing" the thoughts. By this he means to concentrate intently for a moment, then pause, and then start concentrating on it again, continuing to repeat this, all the while taking deep breaths. Long adds that belief and conviction will always bring the best results. The advantages of deep breathing in other connections will be discussed later, and a breathing exercise will be given you which will be helpful in your stopping smoking program.

Dr. James M. Hixson, a Hollywood dentist who is one of the instructors with Hypnosis Symposiums, recommends a short cut in giving auto-suggestion. He advises writing out in detail exactly what you wish to accomplish. Then condense the idea into a sentence or two, omitting details but stating just the result desired. From these sentences select a key word or very brief phrase which includes the entire idea you have first written out. This key word or phrase is to be repeated several times to yourself, after which your thoughts should be diverted to something entirely different. This is all best done while in self-hypnosis.

How the Émily Coué technique can help you.

There was quite an interest during the nineteen-twenties in the use of auto-suggestion for self-benefit, though it was much greater in Europe than in America. Coué, Baudouin, Pierce, and several others wrote books on this subject. Coué operated a clinic on auto-suggestion in Nancy, France, and became world famous because of his success. He was a pharmacist but made a study of the psychology of suggestion. Many people in Europe who followed his methods found them of great value and were benefitted.

Coué came to the United States on a lecture tour but our skeptical newspapermen ridiculed him and scoffed at his ideas so that his tour was a failure. His ideas actually were sound and it was unfortunate that he was so ridiculed.

One of his techniques was to repeat again and again each day the suggestion, "Every day in every way I'm getting better and better." In his earlier work with suggestion, he made use of specific, detailed wordings. Often this was effective, but later he decided that the general, non-specific suggestion, avoiding telling the subconscious how to reach a goal, was better. Such a suggestion would include all that one might be aiming at, not one particular goal. The formula has definite merit.

Coué was the first person to make an exhaustive study of suggestion and its effects. He originated several ideas and laws about suggestion. One he termed the Law of Reversed Effect. If you think, "I'd like to do this but I can't" (a negative thought), the harder you try, the less you are able to do it. This word *try* implies doubt. It's a good word to avoid. When you say "I'll try" about anything, you are really saying that you expect to fail. When attempting anything, it should be approached in a positive way. You are going to quit smoking, not try to quit. Or you are going to cut down on your smoking, not try to cut down.

Using the law of reversed effect.

Here's a good example of this Law of Reversed Effect, to show you how it works. It's a very important law because we encounter it continually in our daily living.

If a 12 foot board, a foot wide, is laid on the ground, you could walk its length while hardly giving it a glance. Placed between two chairs two or three feet above the floor, you could still walk it with no difficulty but with a little more care. Place this same board between the windows of two buildings ten stories from the ground and try to walk it! Fear and doubt would enter and the Law of Reversed Effect would go into action. The walker would probably fall off if he was even able to venture out on the board at all.

Baudouin gives another illustration of this important law. A person learning to ride a bicycle, still unsure of his balance, sees a tree in front of him. Wondering if he can avoid it, he tries to steer away but is sure to run into the tree.

Another example of this law is seen in the case of the person bothered with insomnia. He goes to bed with the negative thought, "I suppose I'll not be able to go to sleep." Then he tries and the harder he tries to go to sleep, the wider awake he becomes. Later, thoroughly fatigued, he stops trying and thinks of something else. Within a few moments he drops off to sleep.

In your program of ending the cigarette habit or cutting down, this law is something to be overcome. You'll be told later how this can be accomplished.

Coué made another wise observation. He said, "When the imagination and the will are in conflict, the imagination will always win." In effect this is saying that the subconscious mind will always win over the conscious part when they are in conflict. It surely is true, yet the conscious part can also influence the inner mind.

Still another of Coué's contributions was what he called the Law of Dominant Effort—an idea always tends toward realization and a stronger emotion will always counteract a weaker one.

SUMMARY

In this chapter you've learned about the laws and rules of suggestion, and of its power. You'll know better how to make auto-suggestions which can be of help to you in your program of stopping smoking. You'll remember to keep suggestions permissive for the most part, though at times you may need to prod your subconscious in a more positive, commanding way. In using suggestion you will apply repetition, the use of visual imagery, suggesting end results but not means, and your motivations for stopping smoking or cutting down will be impressed on your inner mind. Later you'll be given the proper suggestions which will be of most help in carrying out your program so that it becomes relatively easy to rid yourself of the smoking habit.

9

How to Hypnotize Yourself

With a knowledge of both the false ideas and the actual facts about hypnosis, you should readily learn to hypnotize yourself. Employing it in your quitting program or in cutting down on your smoking will make it immeasurably easier for you. Learning self-hypnosis certainly will be of advantage in many other ways as well. That is why I've gone into such detail about hypnosis. Even if you never use it after you have quit smoking for any other purpose than for visits to your dentist, it would be well worth your while.

It probably will be quite easy for you to learn how to do it. Most can do so after a bit of practice. Some will find it more difficult, and a few will fail. You probably will not be one of those who fail but, if so, you can still quit smoking with the method given here, though it may not be quite as easy for you.

In all probability you can learn self-hypnosis by following the method given in this chapter—by making a recording of the induction talk and the suggestions for ending or cutting down on the tobacco habit which follow. However, the easiest and quickest way to learn auto-hypnosis is to be first hypnotized by someone else—a properly qualified physician or psychologist. (By all means stay away from anyone advertising himself as a hypnotist.)

With such help, you may learn self-hypnosis in just one session, or perhaps it will take two or three. If you do not find results in three sessions, you might continue to practice by yourself for a time and eventually succeed, though this is rather doubtful. Probably about one person in twenty will fail, so it is unlikely to be you.

After hypnotizing you, such a practitioner would give you a post-hypnotic suggestion for inducing the state yourself. He would suggest some brief formula for you to follow, both for entering hypnosis and for getting deeper into it. When you follow this formula, you are then carrying out the post-hypnotic suggestion he has given you. With a little practice you should then do well with auto-hypnosis.

A few people are able to go into a very deep state with the first induction attempt. This may be so with you. More likely you'll find yourself at a medium depth, or possibly only at a light state. For most purposes a light one is entirely satisfactory and effective. If childbirth or surgery were intended, the deeper stages would be better.

If you have someone hypnotize you, he could also give you suggestions to help in your quitting or cutting down. The suggestions would be similar to those you will be given here later.

Finding the right person to hypnotize you.

In order to find a physician or psychologist who might help you, try calling your local medical association office, if there is one where you live. Perhaps your own physician may know of a colleague to whom he could send you.

Otherwise you can learn the name of a qualified person by writing one of the three national societies, stating your purpose as to hypnosis. Only by knowing your purpose would the society be able to refer you to the proper person. Be sure to enclose a stamped, self-addressed envelope for reply. If you do not there's no reason why your letter should be answered. These societies are:

The Society for Clinical & Experimental Hypnosis, 353 West 57th St., New York, N.Y. 10019.

The American Society for Clinical Hypnosis, 800 Washington Ave., S.E., Minneapolis, Minn.

The American Society of Psychosomatic Dentistry & Medicine, 964 Delaware Ave., Buffalo 9, N.Y.

Many dentists are familiar with hypnosis. You might find one willing to help you with self-hypnosis, but most would feel that teaching this is hardly a dental matter and prefer to use hypnosis only for dental purposes.

Making a recording.

If you prefer to learn by yourself or are unable to find anyone in your vicinity who could help you, you should make a recording of the induction talk and suggestions which follow later. The recording could be either on tape or by cutting a phonograph record if you do not have a tape recorder. Many stores which sell records and record players have equipment for cutting records and it is easy to make one. The charge is very small. If you do not have either a tape recorder or a record player, you could have some relative or friend read you the words of the induction talk and of the suggestions for controlling the tobacco habit.

Regardless of the method you use, whether listening

to someone read the induction talk, or hearing it played, or going to a professional, you will be hypnotizing yourself. All hypnosis is self-hypnosis. When you listen, just follow all that is said. Then when you practice self-induction, do it in just the way the recording suggests.

How to practice in learning self-hypnosis.

In practicing it is best at first to use some object for eye fixation. This can be almost anything, a doorknob, a picture on the wall, a spot on the wall or ceiling, a light. Probably the best object is a lighted candle. It should be placed in a candlestick or fixed so it can burn down without danger and it should be in a position so you can look at it comfortably, without straining. Watching its flickering flame is very conducive to hypnosis.

You should take a comfortable position where you can relax well, either sitting in a comfortable chair, or lying down. Be sure your clothing is not so tight as to be uncomfortable. It is important for you to be very comfortable in every way.

The real secret in learning hypnosis is in fixing your attention for a moment, or two or three, relaxing as much as possible and letting go. You must let hypnosis come, and not try. Trying seems to hold you back. Follow each suggestion given you. Keep your attention on what is being said and ignore everything else. It makes no difference whether you have sought professional help, are listening to a friend read the induction talk to you, or are hearing it as a recording. The more you can let go, the deeper you'll slip into hypnosis. It would be better to be induced at least twice in this way before beginning to hypnotize yourself.

When you're practicing self-induction you will probably wonder if you are getting results, unless you should reach a very good depth where there is more awareness of being hypnotized. Your mental attitude should be positive rather than doubtful. In your first three practice sessions don't care about results. Just take it for granted that you are hypnotized even though you feel only a bit listless or lethargic. Try not to be analytic about the experience. Just enjoy the relaxation and comfort. Everyone finds being hypnotized is most pleasant.

You'll be going through a learning process. You may do very well the first time you try self-induction and even reach a deep stage. It is more likely for you to be only lightly hypnotized or in a medium state. You'll certainly improve with practice and learn to slip deeper. For the first three practice sessions you should not try to find out how deeply you've gone. It would be discouraging if you found you had not been very deep. With three or four practice sessions you should be doing well and can then learn about depth and make tests. Probably you'll be about as deep as you'll ever learn to go when you've practiced eight or ten times.

Testing the depth of hypnosis you reach.

After your third session you can begin making tests. Of course you could do so sooner if you are certain you're reaching a good depth, as you well may. Then you can find the depth you reach by using our imaginary yardstick and asking your subconscious to measure with it.

Your first test would best be what is termed *arm levitation*. With your arms relaxed, lying beside you or on the arms of your chair (while in hypnosis), concentrate on your right arm. If you are left-handed, use the left. You may have a feeling of heaviness in your arms and legs. Suggest to yourself that all sensation of weight in that arm will quickly leave, will drain away.

Then you could give some such suggestions as these, "My arm is getting lighter and lighter, lighter and lighter. The weight is draining away. My hand will begin to float up into the air, float up toward my face. It will lift higher and higher until my fingers touch my face. The arm will bend at the elbow and the hand float up, higher and higher. Soon it will touch my face."

Your arm will quickly lose all feeling of weight and the hand will start to lift. Perhaps the fingers will move first, then the whole hand and arm begin to lift. Keep repeating the suggestions using your own wording. Don't make any voluntary movement of the arm, but don't hold it back. Your subconscious mind controls the muscles and will move it.

Your hand may begin to float upwards within only a moment or two or it may take a little longer. If it doesn't lift of its own accord within about three minutes, then lift it up several inches and hold it there while you give further suggestions of it floating on up from there.

You'll notice when it first begins to move that it lifts in little jerks. This may continue or the movement may become smoother and more rapid as the arm goes higher. You may be aware of the progress the hand makes or you may find you've lost track of the whole arm and are not sure just where it is as it moves upward. Finally your hand will touch your face and you can then let the arm fall or lower it into any comfortable position.

If this test is successful, you have definitely reached at least a light state of hypnosis. If there is failure, try again in your next practice session and take a little longer in giving your suggestions, repeating them again and again.

Making other tests.

The eye closure test is another which indicates at least a light hypnotic depth when it is successful. With your eyes closed (while in hypnosis) look up towards your forehead. Think to yourself that you are going to count to three and then will be unable to open your eyes. Your suggestions could be about like this, "I'm going to count to three and I'll then be unable to open my eyes. The harder I try to open them, the tighter they'll stick together. One—my eyelids are glueing together, tightly together, sticking fast. Two—it's as though they were welded together now, welded into one piece. I couldn't possibly get them apart. Three—they are locked together now. Tight, tight together." Keep repeating the word *tight* or the word *locked* while you now try to open your eyes. As soon as you find they won't open, stop trying. Give these suggestions slowly, allowing time for them to become effective. Don't hurry.

A handclasp test can be carried out very similarly. With your hands clasped tightly together, fingers interlaced, squeeze your palms tightly together. Then use the same wording for your suggestions, substituting hands for eyes.

How to induce anesthesia.

Another type of test of hypnosis is by production of some phenomenon. The best for this purpose is to induce anesthesia. If your yardstick measurement of depth is about fifteen inches or more, you can probably produce anesthesia. Invoking it in one hand makes a good test, and this is usually called "glove anesthesia." There are various ways of suggesting anesthesia, but with self-hypnosis the following is very effective.

It will help to remove any skepticism and doubt if you understand how anesthesia works physiologically. When pain is stimulated some place the pain nerves carry an electrical impulse to the brain. It must register in the brain or pain is not felt. An injection of a local drug such as novocaine blocks or paralyzes the nerves so the electric impulse doesn't reach the brain. Then you feel only numbness in the area where the injection was made, or the region to which it extends. In hypnotic anesthesia the subconscious probably does the same thing—blocks the impulse from registering in the brain. The nerve is short-circuited.

While in hypnosis, with your eyes closed visualize as though in your head a long row of electric light switches. Above each switch see a little light, each one a different color or shade of color, and all are lit. You can see a red light, a pink one, light blue, dark blue, orange, yellow, all the various colors and shades. Each switch goes to a different part of your body. You can decide for yourself to what part each one goes. In this case, select as to which leads to your hand—right or left depending on your handedness. Let's say you select the switch with the light green light. Imagine you are turning that switch off. In your mind's eye see the light green light go out as you do so.

Usually a numbness is felt in the hand very quickly, but this is not always true and your hand can be completely anesthetized without numbness appearing.

You can suggest, "My hand is becoming more and more numb. I'm going to pinch the hand in a moment. At first I'll pinch lightly. With each pinch the degree of anesthesia will increase. Then I'll pinch as hard as I can but I'll only feel pressure. It will not hurt; there will only be pressure. It will be as if I were pinching a thin leather glove."

When you feel a little numbness, wait a moment for it to increase. Allow about two minutes following your suggestions for anesthesia to develop well. Then start pinching with your other hand. Use light pinches, then harder ones and finally pinch as hard as you can pinch, with your fingernails. You'll feel pressure but should not find it hurting.

Sometimes anesthesia will be partial rather than complete. You may feel a little pain. You've raised the pain threshold, but not to a point of complete anesthesia. Always pinch the other hand—the unanesthetized one—so you can make a comparison. You are almost sure to find this hand hurting much more when you pinch it. If your test shows only partial anesthesia, more practice probably will increase the amount and perhaps then it will be complete.

Success in producing anesthesia depends somewhat on the depth of hypnosis you reach and on your mental attitude. Doubt and skepticism can block results or make them only partial. Your success will be better if you realize that women can go through childbirth with hypnotic anesthesia and feel little or no pain. Also remember that major surgery can be performed with it.

A few years ago I was one of a panel of instructors giving a course in hypnotic methods at a medical college in Kingston, Jamaica. In speaking about hypnotic anesthesia I mentioned that an unusual application of it had been made during the war. When the Japanese captured Singapore they took many prisoners. Toward the end of the war the medical staff in one of the prison camps ran completely out of all drugs and could get no more. Operations had to be performed and two Australian surgeons resorted to hypnosis as the only possible anesthetic available. They performed a number of operations in this way, often major ones. When I told of this, one of the staff physicians at the college rose and said that he had been in that prison camp and had witnessed and taken part in some of these operations.

If you become a good self-hypnosis subject you may find it possible to induce anesthesia merely by direct suggestion. It might be phrased like this, "When I've stroked my right hand three times slowly from my wrist to the fingertips, it will be completely anesthetized. When I pinch it, I'll feel pressure but it won't hurt. It won't bother me." Continue with the suggestion of increased anesthesia with each pinch. Then test as with the other method.

When you can shut off pain in a hand, it can be done in any other area of the body, using different switches. A good time to do this is when visiting your dentist. If you are a woman and might become pregnant, you can readily learn it for childbirth.

Always remember to remove anesthesia. Some time should be set for it to end. In testing, you would remove it as soon as you had completed the test. You could let it remain for several days, if there was such a need, as with a tooth extraction for instance.

When you have learned self-hypnosis and have practiced a few times you should be reaching a fair depth. Making some of these tests, and inducing glove anesthesia will have been helpful in showing you that you are being

successful. Then you are ready to begin making practical
use of self-hypnosis. You can then start your program of
controlling the tobacco habit.

SUMMARY

The easiest way to learn self-induction is to be hypnotized
by some qualified practitioner. He can then teach you
and give you a formula to follow which will act like a
post-hypnotic suggestion when you set to work to hypnotize yourself.

After three or four practice sessions with self-induction,
you can make tests such as hand-levitation, eye-closure,
the handclasp test, etc., and you can induce some phenomenon such an anesthesia. By using the imaginary yardstick technique, you can learn the depth of hypnosis
reached.

10

Your Self-Hypnotic Induction Talk for Recording

Before making a recording of the wording which follows, you should read it over aloud once or twice. By practicing in this way, you'll make a better recording. Keep your voice to a monotone. Make it monotonous. With a little practice you can get a kind of rhythm by slightly accenting a word now and then. Speak quite slowly, and take your time.

If you are going to make a tape recording and also have a record player, you might try to work in some background music. This should be soft and with slow rhythm, heard only faintly as you speak.

Perhaps you know that your own voice never sounds natural to you when you hear it on a recording. It probably would make no difference in results whether you make the recording yourself or have someone else do it. One side of your tape or record could be this induction talk, which also gives you suggestions and a formula to follow for self-hypnosis. On the other side of your tape or record you could record the suggestions which will help you in your quitting smoking or those given for cutting down. These will be given later.

Your induction talk for recording.

When you are going to listen to this recording you should select a time and situation where you won't be interrupted. Take a comfortable position, being sure your clothing is not so tight it would bother you. Select some object at which to gaze, preferably so you'll be looking up at it, perhaps just a spot or a crack on the ceiling. Keep your attention fixed on the voice as you hear it:

"Within a few moments you will be experiencing a degree of relaxation probably greater than you've ever felt before. Of course the more you relax, the more comfortable you'll be. Keep your eyes focused on whatever you are looking at for a little while. Take a good deep breath and then empty your lungs. Let all the air out. Now another deep breath. That's right. Let the air out and take a third deep breath. Then breathe normally. You tend to relax your muscles more with those deep breaths. Follow the words you will be hearing. Pay no attention to any other sounds. Just relax and listen.

"You may notice a tendency for your eyes to blink a little. Let them wink whenever they want to. You'll probably notice the lids beginning to feel heavy. They'll get heavier and heavier, and it will be harder and harder to keep them open. Getting heavy and soon they will want to close. You can let them close at any time. They'll soon be too heavy to hold open. Now take another good deep breath, relax and let go.

"You will soon be feeling a pleasant, listness drowsiness. You may already have begun to notice it. Just a kind of dreamy drowsiness. A good 'I don't care' feeling. As though any problems have been set aside and nothing matters. Your eyes may be winking more now. Just let them close if they have not already closed. Let them close. The lids are so heavy, so awfully heavy. Let them close and stay closed for a while.

"You may begin to feel a heaviness in your arms and legs. Some people instead feel as though they were without weight, just rather floating. It doesn't matter which you feel, either heaviness or so light that you are floating as though on a soft cloud. The dreamy, drowsiness gradually increases.

"You can relax a bit more now. Start with your right leg. Make the muscles tense. Tighten them up, then let them suddenly go loose and limp. Let all the muscles relax from your toes to your ankle, your calf, your thigh and on clear up to your hip. That right leg relaxes now from the toes to your hip.

"Now let the left leg relax in the same way, first making it as tense as you can and then suddenly let it go slack. Your stomach and abdominal muscles can loosen a bit. Then your chest and breathing muscles. Take another deep breath and it will help your whole body to relax more. That's right. And now the muscles of your back can loosen.

"Often we have some tension in our shoulder and neck muscles. Let them relax and go loose and limp. And now let your arms relax, from your shoulders right down to your finger tips. Isn't it pleasant to really relax and let go? Even your facial muscles can relax. Your whole body is relaxed and you are so comfortable. You'll be even more completely relaxed as you let go more and more.

"All tension is draining away now and you can let yourself drift deeper into this comfortable state. It's just what you have done before many, many times without trying. As when you daydream. You'll be learning how to do it intentionally whenever you may want to. And to use it in many ways to your advantage.

"Now suppose you use your imagination for a moment. Imagine you are standing at the top of an escalator such as there are in some stores. If you don't like to ride escalators, imagine you are standing at the top of a staircase instead. See the steps going down in front of you, moving down if it is an escalator. See the railings. I am going to count backwards from ten to zero. As I start to count, imagine you are stepping on the escalator or starting to walk slowly down the staircase. When we reach zero, imagine you've reached the bottom and step off. Just see this in your mind's eye. And as I count, each count will take you deeper. Deeper with each count. Deeper as the steps move down taking you with them, or as you walk slowly down the steps.

"Ten—now you step on the escalator or take your first step down. Go deeper and deeper with each count. Nine—eight—seven—six. Getting deeper now, deeper and deeper. Five—four—three—two. Still deeper. One—and zero. Step off now and keep going still deeper. Each breath you take will take you deeper.

"You might notice your breathing. It probably has changed and is slower and more abdominal—breathing more from the bottom of your lungs. And you are so comfortable. Let go and enjoy going still deeper. Deeper with each breath you take.

"Notice your arms now. Probably they are both so relaxed that they may feel rather heavy. But one of them is going to lose any feeling of heaviness. If you are right-handed, it will be that hand; if left-handed your left. The whole arm will begin to feel lighter, as though all the weight were draining out of it. Draining out the finger tips. It is getting lighter and lighter now. Soon your whole arm will be without weight, as light as a feather. It will begin to lift up, to lift up. Your hand will begin to float up toward your face. It is getting still lighter now and you'll soon notice the hand itself begin to lift, to float up. Perhaps it has already begun. It will float up, higher and higher, lift up toward your face until it touches.

"The arm begins to bend at the elbow, bending so that the hand lifts and floats up, up higher. If it has not yet begun to float up by itself, lift your hand a few inches, bending the elbow a little and then let it float there.

"Now your hand is floating up, floating higher, higher and higher. It will continue until it touches your face someplace. Floating higher, still higher. Moving a bit faster now. It will keep on lifting until it touches. The higher the hand goes, the deeper you'll go. The deeper you go, the higher the hand will go. As it touches your face, you can go still deeper.

"The hand will keep on lifting until it touches your face. Then it can go down to some comfortable position. Keep on drifting deeper, enjoying the comfortable relaxation. Go deeper and deeper with every breath. In a moment you'll be able to feel your fingers touching your face. Then you can lower your hand.

"You hear every word that is said. You are aware of everything. Just let go still more and drift still deeper. The deeper you go the more comfortable and pleasant it is. Things probably seem a bit dreamy and drowsy to you now. Nothing seems to matter. It's as though all cares were set aside and nothing matters. You are so comfortable, so relaxed and comfortable.

"Each time you listen to these words you'll be able to go deeper into this pleasant state, but no one will be able to hypnotize you unless you are willing and permit it. With experience you can go as deep as you would like to go. All tension has drained away and you are completely relaxed now. Let yourself drift still deeper. Deeper and deeper with each breath.

"All hypnosis is really auto-hypnosis. By carrying out ideas suggested to you, you hypnotize yourself. You merely respond to these suggestions. Of course you can respond to your own suggestions. Your subconscious mind will accept any suggestion you give it as for your benefit. After you learn to hypnotize yourself you'll wish to stop smoking, or perhaps just to cut down on your smoking, to reduce the number of cigarettes you'll be smoking. This inner part of your mind will help you with this, whether your goal is to stop smoking or only to reduce the amount of your smoking. You'll find that you can readily do this.

"Now you are going to learn how to hypnotize yourself at any time you may want to do so. There's no danger in self-hypnosis except for one thing which can easily be prevented. That is the tendency to slip spontaneously into hypnosis when you are driving a car. This frequently happens and is sometimes a dangerous situation, for you are not as alert then as you should be and you might have an accident. At no time when you are driving a car or controlling any other kind of vehicle will it be possible for you to go into hypnosis, or to fall into normal sleep. You will never fall asleep or slip into hypnosis when you are at the controls of any kind of vehicle. At such a time you will stay completely alert and wide awake.

"In learning to hypnotize yourself you'll follow a very similar way of doing it to what you have just been experiencing. I'll give you a simple formula to follow and you will remember it. You'll follow this formula exactly, remembering every part of it. You will make yourself comfortable, just as you have done here. The first three times you practice hypnotizing yourself select some object at which you can look to fix your attention for two or three minutes. After you have practiced a few times, you need not continue doing this, but can merely close your eyes as you begin.

"You probably will not need to say anything aloud; you merely think the suggestions you will be giving yourself. But some people do better if they say the words aloud. You can experiment with this to see if it is true with you. You should select a key word or a phrase which you will say to yourself and this will let you drift immediately into hypnosis, as you repeat it three times slowly. This can be any word or phrase you would like to use. A good one is the phrase 'relax now.' Such a word or phrase will have no effect on you at all unless you are intentionally using it in hypnotizing yourself. It will be ineffective except when you mean it to hypnotize you.

"Repeat this three times very slowly to yourself. At the same time lift one of your hands and touch your face with it. Use your right hand if right-handed, the left if left-handed. Lift it voluntarily, touch your face, then lower the arm and hand to a comfortable position. As you think or speak this word or phrase and at the same time lift your hand to your face, you will slip at once into hypnosis.

"You will want to go into as deep a state as possible, so think to yourself, 'Now I'm going deeper.' Just as you have done here, imagine the escalator or staircase and step on it while you count backwards from ten to zero, just as I have counted. Count slowly. Each count will take you deeper and deeper. In your practicing repeat this two or even three times, as though you were going down different levels. Each time you do this, it will take you deeper. After a few practices, you need only go through it once, as with practice you will be doing better and better and going deeper.

"To relax still more, repeat what you did here in relaxing your body. Start at your feet. Think of the various groups of muscles, relaxing your legs, your trunk, your arms, just as you did here. The more you relax, the deeper you tend to go. The deeper you go, the more you relax. Now and then take a deeper breath, which helps you still further to relax. Take one now and go still deeper.

"While you are self-hypnotized if anything should happen so you should awaken—the phone ringing, or a real emergency like a fire—you will be wide awake instantly. You would awaken instantly and be fully alert.

"Otherwise, to awaken yourself you need only think to yourself when you are ready to awaken, 'Now I'm going to wake up.' Then count slowly to three, or to five if you prefer, counting very slowly. Tell yourself then that you are completely wide awake. You will always awaken refreshed, feeling very relaxed, and clear-headed. You'll always feel wonderfully well on awakening.

"You will be able to use hypnosis for many beneficial purposes. It will be helpful in your program of quitting smoking, or in cutting down, whichever you plan to do. You can utilize it in many other ways. Whenever you give yourself suggestions, the inner part of your mind is to accept them, to realize that they are for your benefit, and it is to carry them out as best it can.

"As you practice self-induction you will be able to go

deeper into hypnosis each session for a time. You will relax more and slip deeper each time, as you learn how
pleasant and comfortable it is to be in hypnosis.

"Sometimes time seems to pass very quickly while you
are hypnotized. Sometimes there is a tendency to drop off
into a normal sleep from hypnosis, especially if you are
tired. You can prevent this with suggestion to yourself
that you will stay in hypnosis until ready to awaken yourself. You can even set a time for you to awaken, or state
to yourself a certain number of minutes at the end of
which time your subconscious will awaken you. Your subconscious can time it accurately and will then cause you
to awaken, either at the moment set, or at the end of the
period of time you've set.

"Having learned to hypnotize yourself, you will never
lose the ability. You'll always remember the formula you
are to follow and will be able to hypnotize yourself at any
time you use it. However, you should remember to use it
now and then to keep in good practice.

"Now you will awaken. When I have counted to five,
you will be wide awake, refreshed, relaxed, feeling wonderfully well. You'll be completely wide awake when I've
counted to five. ONE—now you are beginning to wake up.
TWO—coming awake. THREE—coming wider and wider
awake. FOUR—almost awake now. FIVE—fully wide
awake, now. Wide awake. Eyes open and wide awake.
Wide awake and fully alert."

Using this induction talk.

Before attempting self-hypnosis, it would be well to
listen and respond to this recording twice. Then begin
practicing on self-hypnosis. Of course if you feel sure you
have been quite deeply hypnotized the first time you hear

this recording, or if you have help with induction by a professional man, then you can begin self-hypnosis practice at once.

In practicing you cannot do it too often or harm yourself in any way. Practice at least three times during the next week after you play this recording. Then you will be ready to begin putting your program into effect to control the tobacco habit. Remember that you can use this induction talk by having someone read it to you if it is not possible to record it. In this case whoever is helping you should read it over at least twice before using it with you for an actual induction. And remember, it is you who will be hypnotizing yourself. The operator is only a guide. In this situation it should be read slowly, the voice kept to a monotone.

In learning about hypnosis and how to hypnotize yourself you may become very enthusiastic and wish to share this experience with others, your family or friends. If they wish to learn auto-hypnosis, it is quite all right, but do not use your new knowledge and practice on other people. There's no danger of misusing hypnosis with yourself but unless you have had proper training in psychology or medicine and in the uses of hypnosis, confine your hypnotizing to self-hypnosis. In all probability you would have no trouble and anyone can readily learn to induce hypnosis, but you might inadvertently do something or say something which could cause trouble or be harmful. Also, you do not know the condition of another person's mind, or how depressed or disturbed he might be. Hypnosis might be definitely contraindicated and you would not recognize this. So refrain from becoming a "parlor hypnotist." Use hypnosis to benefit yourself, but it's not a plaything.

SUMMARY

You now have an induction talk which you can use as a recording or can have someone read to you. By following the suggestions given, you should be able to become hypnotized and to reach a good depth. You are given suggestions which include a formula for you to follow in order to hypnotize yourself. It is a brief one and easily remembered. In practicing, do not omit anything, but follow it exactly. You are also given suggestions as to awakening yourself. Of course there is never any difficulty in awakening. You are now ready to begin practicing self-hypnosis.

You may be tempted to use your new knowledge about hypnosis in hypnotizing some friend or member of your family. Don't become a parlor hypnotist. Dangers are minimal but there are some and you should take no risks. With self-hypnosis there's no danger of doing anything harmful to yourself.

11

Your Program for Stopping Smoking

A program to help the light smoker stop smoking will be a bit different from that for the heavy smoker or addict. Basically it will be much the same but, if you are a light smoker, some details can be omitted. Many light smokers will have little difficulty quitting, but others will not find it so easy without some help. A program for the smoker who wants to cut down rather than stop will be given later.

In any program, self-hypnosis is not essential but will make the quitting process far easier, with the chance of failure very much reduced. Your first step is to learn self-hypnosis. For this probably three or four practice sessions will be all you'll need. You may learn in only one or two sessions, if you happen to be an excellent hypnotic subject. More practice may be necessary for some. When you are sure you are able to hypnotize yourself, you can arrange a schedule for breaking yourself of the tobacco habit.

Setting up your program.

When should you stop smoking? You are about to deal with a well-formed habit. Therefore it is best to interrupt it at some break in your usual living habits. Undoubtedly one of the best times to stop smoking is when you have a cold or the flu, for tobacco tastes horrible at such a time and there's little satisfaction in smoking. For a woman, pregnancy is an ideal time to quit, for this condition often makes tobacco taste bad and the craving is less. There may even be aversion to tobacco. However you need not wait for an illness or pregnancy!

If you plan to take a trip of any kind, vacation or business trip, or if you plan anything different from your usual activities, that would be a good time to set for quitting. In deciding on your "Emancipation day"—let's call it E-day—you don't have to put it off if nothing unusual is in prospect. Let it be set for a weekend, making Friday the last day when you'll smoke.

Your program should start five or six days before E-day. This is to be after you've learned self-hypnosis. Tell your physician of your plan and ask him to prescribe for you whatever tranquilizer he thinks will be best suited for you. There are many kinds and, knowing your case and your physical condition, he will know which one would be best for you. Be sure to let the doctor know that you also will be taking another drug, too, as described in the following paragraphs.

Most tranquilizers have a cumulative effect and it is a few days before their effect is noticed. Hence you should begin taking the one given you at least five days before E-day. Your doctor can advise on this point. Discontinue this drug when you've not smoked for two weeks, provided that you are not feeling any excessive nervous tension. If you have found it easy to quit, you might stop after the first week of no smoking. It's best to cut the dosage over a period of three or four days rather than to stop taking the drug suddenly.

The other drug is to be one of the anti-smoking drugs which require no prescription. There are several on the market under different trade names, the main ingredient being lobeline sulphate. Be sure to use the lozenge type which you hold in your mouth rather than a pill to swallow.

The advertising for this drug is misleading, with wonderful results claimed. It sounds as if all you need do to stop smoking is to take a few of these pills or lozenges and you'll never want to smoke again. The drug derives from "Indian tobacco" and is chemically similar to nicotine but without its bad effects. It serves only as a substitute for nicotine. It has no effect on any psychological craving to smoke. Taking it is merely one slight help for you, tending to lessen withdrawal symptoms somewhat. Start taking the drug after your dinner the night before your E-day. Continue with one after each meal for about a week. By that time all the nicotine will be out of your system.

Something else you should have on hand for E-day is a stock of chewing gum or Life-savers, Flavettes, or any other kind of lozenge which you may like. You can buy peppermint and other flavors. These are to be used only for the first few days after you quit smoking. Probably you'll not need them after the third day. They will serve instead of cigarettes to satisfy to some extent the oral craving which you probably will have for the first few days.

Another purchase you might make is one which seems to be helpful to some people—an imitation cigarette. They are sold in most drug stores. Like lozenges or gum, they are intended to help satisfy this need to put something in your mouth. It can also help satisfy another need experienced by some ex-smokers. That is, it can be used to twiddle between your fingers, giving you something to do with your hands and helping to relieve nervous tension in this way.

All of these accessories are only for the heavy smoker or the addict to have on hand and use. If you smoke less than a pack a day, you may need none of these "crutches." Possibly gum or lozenges could help, but the other things are unnecessary.

Starting your program.

To begin with, take a sheet of paper and write down every possible motive of which you can think for stopping smoking. Here is a list of some, just listed briefly. Elaborate on them as to your own particular case. You can probably find still others which would apply to you.

1. Your general health—to avoid the possibility of developing lung cancer, pulmonary or heart conditions.
2. To feel better, free of coughs, shortness of breath.
3. To have more energy.
4. To sleep better.
5. To have less nervous tension, to relax better.
6. To save all the money and expense involved in smoking.

7. To end the burning of clothing, furniture and the hazards of fire.
8. For cleanliness—to be rid of dirty ashtrays, soiled clothing, obnoxious odors, spilled ashes, etc.
9. To set a good example for children so they will not imitate you and smoke when they grow older—if they are older and smoking, to help them stop.
10. To have better mental powers, a more alert mind, and better concentration.
11. To have a fresh tasting mouth, whiter teeth, pleasant breath.
12. To have food taste better.
13. To have things smell better.
14. To be able to prove your ability to overcome the smoking habit, with the good sense of accomplishment which results.

Writing out all these motives and advantages in ending the tobacco habit is intended to stimulate and strengthen your desire to quit. The stronger your desire to stop smoking, the more you want to quit, the easier it will be for you to accomplish it. It is a very important part of your program to change the idea that you *should* quit into a strong desire to stop. You must really want to stop rather than merely feel you should.

Read over your list of reasons at least three times before your E-day and again during the evening of that first day when you are free of smoking. Impress on yourself all these advantages. Read it over again each evening of the first three days after you've become an ex-smoker, and again a few days later. Preparing and reading over this list is a step in the program of all types of smokers.

Breaking your old habits in smoking.

Also for all types of smokers are these revisions in your smoking habits. Change your brand. If you have been using filtertips, buy a brand without the tips. If you've been smoking king size cigarettes, change to the regular size. If your brand has been mild, change to strong ones. If yours have been strong, turn now to the mildest you can find. If you like and use menthol-flavored cigarettes, change to those without menthol.

For the two days just before your E-day, you should double the number of cigarettes you've been smoking, or at least increase the number greatly. If you've been a "pack-a-dayer," smoke two packs or even more. If you've been smoking two packs now make it four. If a real addict and smoking more than two packs, you must smoke at least two extra packs.

The idea in this is to make you thoroughly fed-up with the taste of tobacco. With this program of increasing your number, you will be! You'll find you really must force yourself to smoke so much, but be sure you do it. This means you will be smoking when you don't feel the need or desire, as well as when you do.

There's another reason for this step. Dr. Knight Dunlap is the greatest authority on habits. According to Dunlap the best way to break any habit is to consciously exaggerate it very considerably. It works.

Let's say you will be smoking three packs a day on this speeded up smoking. Be sure you've smoked at least one pack before lunchtime. By then you'll find the last ones do not taste good and you haven't enjoyed them. After lunch you probably will enjoy one. Smoke a second within ten minutes of finishing that one. By five o'clock be sure you've finished the second pack. Start on the third then and get in at least two or even three before dinner. More if your dinner hour is late. After dinner make sure you finish off the entire third pack before going to bed. You may have to smoke three or four in the last half hour to do it.

By this time your mouth will be tasting like an old leather shoe, or even worse. That formerly pleasant odor of tobacco smoke may resemble burning hair instead!

You undoubtedly will have to force yourself with this stepped up program of smoking. Don't slight it. The second day of this will be worse and you'll want to call it off. Don't. It is a most helpful step prior to quitting. As you smoke the last one before going to sleep the second night, you'll really be fed-up. Next morning, with you now an ex-smoker as of the night before, you'll hardly miss that first one. After breakfast your old habit will make you think of reaching for your usual cigarette. Right then remember how the last one tasted. How awful it was! Think to yourself, "Never again. I'm glad I'm through." Then divert your mind to something else or start some kind of activity.

Committing yourself to quitting.

When you have decided on your E-day, announce it to your family, your friends and your associates. Spread the word—shout it from the housetops. By doing this you are committing yourself and would, of course, feel ashamed if you failed to stop smoking. It gives you still another motive *not* to fail, but to go through with your program.

Some who quit think it helps to make a bet with a friend who is also quitting at the same time. If you think it will help, such a wager could do you some good, particularly if it is an amount that you definitely would not want to lose.

It's very helpful to have a "companion in misery,"—someone who will be quitting at the same time you do. If your spouse smokes, it's an ideal arrangement for both to stop at the same time. It makes it much easier and you'll bolster each other in talking over the problem and how you get along with your program.

Using self-hypnosis in your program.

You will have learned self-hypnosis before deciding on your E-day. Now you are ready to begin applying what you've learned. You can use the suggestion recording or you can have someone read the suggestions to you, after you've hypnotized yourself. If you have decided for some reason not to use self-hypnosis or have been unable to hypnotize yourself, you can still listen to the suggestions even though not hypnotized.

A few people who have read this far may still be a bit fearful, even with the assurance that self-hypnosis is perfectly safe. However, suggestions are effective whether we are hypnotized or not, when they are heard repeatedly. Advertising proves this. Under hypnosis we do become more highly suggestible. Then suggestion is super-charged and becomes much more potent. Hypnosis certainly will make it much easier for you to be rid of the tobacco habit, but many people of course have stopped smoking without being hypnotized.

Influencing your subconscious through suggestions.

Suggestion is one of the best ways of influencing the inner part of the mind. The subconscious controls much of our behavior, but it can, in turn, also be influenced so that it will aid us in accomplishing something we want to do. Hence we use hypnosis and the hypersuggestibility which accompanies it to help with the quitting process.

When you read the suggestions for recording given in a later chapter, you'll see that they are aimed first at modifying or eliminating the desire to smoke. They will serve to bolster your determination. These suggestions will make you impervious to others who may be smoking in your presence, impervious when urged to smoke or offered a cigarette, impervious to advertising about cigarettes, unaffected by any negative suggestions or ideas which may be given you by others.

When you've set your E-day, you should begin listening to these recorded suggestions, playing them over each day. Probably the best time is during the evening, taking a few moments when you can be alone and uninterrupted. Continue playing the recording each day for the first three days after quitting, or longer if you feel it necessary. You may want to play it again a week or two weeks later. You can always supplement these recorded suggestions with some of your own which may fit your particular case or situation more exactly.

In using self-hypnosis in your program there is another advantage in that you learn to relax better. You can't be tense while you are relaxed. Tension and relaxation are opposites. If you have less tension, the need for a cigarette will be less. Continuing to use self-hypnosis after you've stopped smoking will greatly lessen nervous tension and therefore decrease the need or desire for a cigarette.

Organizing a group of friends who wish to quit smoking.

It was mentioned that it's helpful to have your spouse or some friend quit smoking when you stop. Perhaps you can find another couple who also want to quit. If you discuss this with your circle of friends and acquaintances you can probably find several who would be glad to join you in organizing a "Smokers Anonymous" group, like Alcoholics Anonymous.

In England the government has sponsored "stop smoking clinics" in several cities, in connection with the socialized medicine program in effect in that country. Groups of twenty-five to thirty people who wish to stop smoking are organized, with a physician presiding. Meetings are held one evening each week for a number of weeks. Every effort is made to promote strong desires to end the smoking habit, and lectures are given as to the illnesses which can result from cigarette smoking. Films or slides of such cases are projected for the benefit of those who are participating. Results in these clinics have been very gratifying, ranging from 50% to 70% successful, and with few relapses. Others in these group classes have been able to reduce their consumption of cigarettes and keep it cut down. In Sweden also the government has maintained such clinics.

In many European countries the tobacco business is a government monopoly. Tobacco is not taxed, the government makes prices such that there is a great profit instead. But advertising is restricted or even eliminated, as in Italy, for instance.

If you can interest some of your friends in organizing a group and setting up a program for quitting, all should either read this book or should arrange for a group leader to discuss the methods given here for ending the habit. In preliminary meetings self-hypnosis can be learned by each of the participants. Best results will undoubtedly come if your group numbers at least eight and up to fifteen or sixteen.

Your first meeting should be organizational, with a leader chosen who will preside at the next meeting and some later ones. Later others, too, can act as leader so that the original leader can have opportunities to participate instead of lead.

At the first meeting your program should be laid out and discussed. This will be given in detail at the end of this chapter. Either at this meeting or the next the leader should act as the hypnotist and should read the induction recording. As an alternate procedure a recording could be made and all could listen but the results might be better if the leader read the induction talk.

For some reason, when a group induction is made, most everyone in the group will become hypnotized readily and more deeply than with individual inductions. Perhaps there's an unconscious feeling of greater safety in the group. There certainly is a better acceptance of the induction suggestions. You will probably find every one in the group will become hypnotized and many will be able to reach a very good depth.

If you organize such a group with the members all planning to quit smoking, you'll undoubtedly have great success. Each one seems to bolster the other in his resolves. Each feels that he mustn't let the group down by failing, and a feeling of shame at the thought of failing before the rest of the group acts to prevent failure. Undoubtedly organizing a group and working together is the very best way of applying the measures given here to stop smoking. Of course you can stop on your own, individually. But it's easier with a group.

All members of the group should learn self-hypnosis so that they can supplement group work by individual efforts in applying the quitting program. The first leader might best be a man, but in some later sessions have a woman act as the leader and give the induction talk. Some will respond better to a male operator, others to a female. As a matter of fact women make excellent hypnotists. Probably the subject unconsciously assigns the female operator a mother role.

The first two group meetings should be mainly for organization and to learn to become hypnotic subjects. Then practice will permit all to learn self-hypnosis. Meetings should be held once a week, and can be continued as long as it seems desirable. Actually only five or six sessions would be enough for most in any group, but it might be advisable and interesting to carry them further. Those who respond the best may drop out before others, or may find the meetings so interesting that they continue to attend.

A group program.

Each individual in the group will follow the personal program given in the next chapter that will fit his needs, whether as a light smoker or a heavy one.

First meeting.

Discuss the general plan. Someone who has read this book should tell briefly how hypnosis is to be used to aid each member of the group in quitting. Probably several will have read the book and a general discussion can be had about the program which is to be followed. Be sure to discuss the usual misconceptions about hypnosis so that any fears about it can be removed.

Decide on a leader for this and for the next session. It would be best if he has read the book and is familiar with it. Set a date for the future meetings, probably keeping the same night each week that is most convenient for all. If time allows, the leader can read the induction talk given in Chapter Ten. Follow this with a general discussion of what has been experienced. No tests as to the depth reached by individuals should be made, nor any hypnotic phenomena induced other than as given in the induction talk.

Second meeting.

This meeting is largely to help the members develop hypnosis and then in practicing by themselves to learn self-hypnosis. The recorded suggestions for self-hypnosis should be read to the group by the operator. When all have been awakened, there should be a few moments spent practicing self-hypnosis. At either this session or the next the suggestions for quitting smoking should also be read to the group while all are hypnotized.

Decide on E-day at this session, setting it either for the day of the next meeting or for the next one after that.

Each member follows his individual daily program in the meantime.

Third or E-day meeting.

Group induction by a different operator. Quitting suggestions given again. General discussion of how the day has gone. Those who may not have been as successful as others will find that they can do as well on the next and following days.

If the group maintains its interest, meetings can be continued over the next four weeks to the advantage of most members. Those who have been completely successful can encourage others who may have not been able to stop completely during the first week or two, but it is quite likely that all will have stopped.

SUMMARY

When you have learned self-hypnosis you are ready to start your program of ending the tobacco habit. You should set up your E-day—Emancipation-day—five or six days ahead. Obtain a tranquilizer drug prescription from your physician, lay in a supply of gum or some kind of lozenge, and an anti-smoking drug (lobeline sulphate) You may want to buy an imitation cigarette which you can put in your mouth as a substitute for a real one. A cigarette holder could serve the same purpose.

Your first step is then to write out all the reasons and motives you have for quitting smoking. Change your brand of cigarette for this five or six day period. For the last two days before E-day, increase the number of cigarettes smoked to approximately double the usual number, so you'll be fed-up by E-day. Let your friends know you are quitting. Using self-hypnosis, listen to the suggestions which you will have recorded, or have someone read them.

It will be helpful if you enlist someone else in quitting with you, perhaps your spouse, or a friend. Much better is to organize a group of friends all of whom wish to stop smoking. A schedule of meetings can be arranged, leaders chosen and a program followed by the group. Each member would also follow the individual daily program given in the next chapter which would best fit his needs.

12

Your Program After E-Day

Until you find the tobacco habit completely whipped and the desire to smoke gone, start each day by drinking a glass of orange or some other kind of fruit juice immediately on awakening. This should be done as soon as you get out of bed, preferably before dressing. As soon as you have dressed, brush your teeth. When you've finished your breakfast brush your teeth again and use a mouthwash. If you have not been using one, use hydrogen peroxide. This procedure will make it much easier for you to forego that after breakfast cigarette.

Overcoming desire to smoke.

Of course in quitting, individuals will vary considerably in response. The light smoker and some others, even an occasional addict, may find all desire has vanished on E-day, with no further need to smoke. Of course everyone would like this effect. Perhaps you'll have it.

More likely the average person will find a desire for a smoke popping up at times. It is most likely to be strongest following a meal or when you are having a cup of coffee or an alcoholic drink. Thought of smoking will come into your mind at other times, too. Another situation where the desire may be strong is when you are under some emotion, particularly if upset about something, or if embarrassed.

If you had ever taken the time and trouble to study the pattern of your smoking, you would have found a cycle involved. In all probability you developed a wish to smoke after some definite length of time following your last cigarette. This cycle would be modified by mealtimes, by emotions being stirred up, by certain happenings in your daily routine such as coffee breaks, watching TV, and various other things. When you've stopped smoking, some of the urges to smoke will be timed in this cycle.

What to do when you have the urge to smoke.

When the urge to smoke rears its nasty head, you must kill it in some way. If you nurse the thought, dwelling on it, wishing you could yield to the desire, think how good it would be to have that soul-satisfying drag—you're sunk. Very likely you'll reach for a cigarette.

On the other hand you can rid yourself of these urges when they pop up. When such a thought comes to mind, immediately counteract it. You can smother it by thinking, "No! I'm through smoking. I don't need a cigarette. It would taste horrible."

You must also divert your mind to something else. Pop a Lifesaver or some gum into your mouth—fast. Think of something else—anything—that blonde, your golf game, anything at all. If you divert your thoughts, you'll find the desire to smoke has disappeared.

Practice a Yoga breathing exercise.

Another technique to use when that devilish urge comes is to sit down and practice a breathing exercise. It will serve a double purpose. In doing the exercise you are distracting your mind from the idea of smoking, and you are also clearing your lungs and hyperventilating slightly, taking in more oxygen.

This breathing exercise is valuable. It is very simple and you can learn it quickly, just practicing two or three times. It is a Yoga breathing exercise, although in Yoga practice it is carried on much longer than for our purpose here. In the Occident we pay little or no attention to the way we breath, though you've probably heard somewhere that deep breathing is good for you. In Yoga a study has been made of breathing and various exercises have been developed. Great claims are made as to the benefits. Yogins believe these exercises stimulate what they call *prana*, bringing life force into the body.

Our exercise has been called the 4-8-4 exercise. With your forefinger hold the left side of your nostril closed, pressing firmly on that side of your nose. Inhale slowly, filling your lungs. This should take four seconds. You can time it by counting as does a photographer in timing seconds—thinking "a thousand one, a thousand two, a thousand three, a thousand four." That will be four seconds.

You breathe in through the right nostril for four seconds, hold it for eight, then close that nostril and breathe out through the left nostril, taking four seconds. Then breathe in through the same (left) nostril four seconds, hold for eight, and out through the right nostril four seconds. That completes the exercise, or one cycle of it. In through the right nostril, hold, out through the left; in through the left, hold, out through the right.

In Yoga practice this is repeated through several cycles but for our purpose you need only go through it one or two cycles. Of course if you wish, you can continue and will find it very stimulating. You'll have a nice feeling of well-being thereafter. You might continue for a total of no more than six complete cycles. With some practice, you could do eight cycles, but do not overdo this as you are hyperventilating.

Will you gain weight when you quite smoking?

Popularly it is thought that the person who stops smoking will overeat and gain weight. There is some truth to this, for overeating is another form of oral satisfaction. It may be a substitute for smoking. However, it doesn't have to be, and you certainly do not have to gain weight. Even with such a tendency it is easily avoided. Knowing that it's a possibility, you can take steps to prevent. In the first place, the realization can cause you to watch your diet. Make it a point to avoid the fattening types of food for a time after E-day. This means the carbohydrates in particular, the starches, sweets, and animal fats.

The tendency to overeat, if present, can also be curbed by making it a habit to keep food in your mouth for a longer time while eating. In other words, chew each mouthful longer. We have tastebuds so food will taste good to us. Smoking has numbed them but it will not be long after your E-day when you will notice your food is tasting better. It will have more flavor. If you chew your food longer, savoring each mouthful, you'll not overeat. If you bolt your food with little chewing, you'll continue to stuff more into your mouth, which means more calories and the tendency to bulge at the waistline. Almost every obese person bolts his food rather than chewing properly.

Your self-hypnosis and suggestion program will also be a way of curbing any tendency to overeat. In your recorded suggestions some are worded to help control your appetite. You can supplement these with other suggestions of your own.

Get rid of temptation.

The evening before E-day you must get rid of any cigarettes you may have left, following your excessive smoking of that day. If your thinking is such that you believe you should have some on hand to fall back on if absolutely necessary, then you are not ready to stop smoking. You haven't made up your mind that you can quit. If you are going to *try* to stop you'll have no success. That word means you expect to fail. Having even one cigarette available will be a temptation. If you have none available, you can't smoke.

Your mental attitude.

With your ability to hypnotize yourself and use suggestion, you should be fully prepared for E-day. But unless you have rid yourself of most of your doubts, unless you have decided that you can and will be an ex-smoker, you will have trouble. You may be able to stop smoking, but you'll have a battle. Your attitude should be, "of course I can stop." In all probability you'll be amazed at how easy it has been when you look back after a couple of weeks of not smoking.

Almost anyone who has ever stopped smoking, whether with these methods or with others, reports the first three days without smoking as being the worst time. After that you are "over the hump." You'll have to combat occasional desires to smoke for a few more days but it's much easier and the wish comes less frequently with every passing day. When a week has passed, it's still easier. At the end of two weeks you seldom have to combat such urges.

By this time you are patting yourself on the back, thrusting out your chest. You look patronizingly at those poor misguided mutts of your acquaintance, and even strangers, whom you see smoking. It's too bad they haven't seen the light as you did, and shown their great strength of character by quitting. Well, you're entitled to gloat, but don't make yourself obnoxious to your friends who still smoke.

Danger signals along the way.

In my investigation of the tobacco habit I've been rather surprised at the number of people who have told me, "Oh, I can quit smoking. I quit for three months (or a year) and it wasn't hard to do."

If a person goes to the trouble to quit, why would he ever start smoking again? Apparently some people can stop readily. They have not become victims of the habit. They probably are not smoking excessively. They do not think smoking in their case is harmful when not excessive. Probably it is not very harmful, although we all certainly would be better off if we did not smoke.

Sometimes there is something else involved. With heavier smokers who have been able to stop and have then started again, there seems to have come a time approximately two or three months after they quit smoking when curiosity develops. What would a cigarette taste like now? Of course he has stopped and has no real desire to smoke, but what would one be like?

It's almost as though the Old Nick himself was standing behind this ex-smoker, whispering in his ear. If he dwells on this thought of what one would be like, he'll try one. He's off to the races. He's a smoker again. With heavy or addicted smokers, it's something like alcoholism. They say there's one drink between the alcoholic and the gutter. It's much the same with the heavy smoker. There's one cigarette between being an ex-smoker and an addict again.

This same situation seems to arise at the end of about a year after quitting smoking. It's the same story. There comes this thought of what one would taste like. Try one, and away you go again.

If you are forewarned about these two danger periods, you'll thumb your nose at that shadowy form with hoofs and horns standing behind you. You know what cigarettes were like and particularly what the first one you smoked did to you. Remember how sick it made you—dizzy and nauseated. Think of that effect and you won't want to try one.

This writer's experience in ending the cigarette habit.

I have been a fairly heavy smoker for many, many years—more years than I like to think about. I began my last year in high school. While engaged in athletics in college I would stop, though my last year I failed to do so.

In recent years I've helped many people stop smoking when they came to me for help. I made no effort myself to stop. I didn't want to quit. As more reports about the danger to health from cigarette smoking appeared in the press and in scientific journals, more people came to me for help. I began to feel a little uneasy myself. Perhaps I should stop. I told myself I could easily do it, but there was a doubt there.

It did seem ridiculous for me to keep on smoking while telling others how bad it was for them—then practically blowing smoke in the person's face. So I stopped. I did well the first day. Of course I had to have one before breakfast, and I ended by having one after all three meals, but that was only a total of four. The rest of the day I spent thinking about smoking. Every few moments my hand went into the pocket where I had kept cigarettes. I had thrown away a partial pack the night before, but I knew there were some in a dish which were kept for visitors. It was four of these I'd sneaked.

To make the tale a brief one, I lasted three days, but couldn't get through a single day without smoking. I perspired. I felt anxious and was jittery and irritable. I couldn't keep my mind off smoking. So I gave up and started again. I would help others but quitting was something for others, not for me.

As a psychologist my failure caused me to think a bit. I could see my rationalizations as being just that. I began to study this tobacco problem and how best to whip it. I had relied mainly on hypnotic suggestion when dealing with those who came for help in stopping, and it usually was successful. I now added other techniques such as you have now learned.

When I prepared to write this book I had read the Surgeon General's Committee report. I had known the dangers before, but reading this report rather awakened me. If I was going to write a book on ending the tobacco habit, it was imperative for me to follow my own advice and quit. So I applied the methods I had worked out.

This time the result was entirely different from my previous experience. It was remarkably easy. No will-power involved. (I still doubt if there is such a thing.) Determination was needed, and I had it this time. I had changed my mental attitude. This time I really wanted to quit—wanted strongly to kick the habit.

I had thought over and written out all my incentives and motivations and had added one not present before. Now I had a young son and I didn't want him to grow up and smoke. Almost surely he would be a smoker if I set him the example.

No miracle happened. There were times when I wanted to smoke even after a month had passed, though it was very rare by then. Each time I counteracted the idea when it appeared. I used the 4-8-4 breathing exercise and distracted my mind. After meals was the worst time. The urge quickly disappeared and even E-day was surprisingly easy. Self-hypnosis was most helpful both in preparation for E-day and in the days following. After the first week I didn't even bother any more with hypnosis or further suggestions.

From my previous horrible experience in trying to break the habit I would class myself as having been an addict, although I did not seem to smoke as much as do most addicts. A carton of cigarettes lasted me about eight days, sometimes even nine or ten. Evidently I smoked an average of about twenty-five a day. When I first had tried to stop, I went through withdrawal symptoms and couldn't quit. For me, that's addiction, whether or not it conforms to the accepted technical definition of addiction.

Having been able to end the habit so easily myself and having found the methods I used so helpful in my own case and in helping others, I feel sure you will also have much the same results.

A daily program for the light or medium types of smokers.

The light smoker can follow a modified procedure, as is given here. Most moderate or medium class of smokers can also use this program. A few in the medium class may need to use the schedule given for the heavy smoker. In the next chapter a program is given for smokers who only wish to cut down rather than to stop entirely. For all three programs self-hypnosis should first have been learned.

On the first day, with E-day set up for three days later.

1. Buy any supplies you may need—gum, lozenges, mouthwash.
2. Tell your friends and acquaintances you are stopping on your E-day.
3. Change the brand you are smoking.
4. Write out your list of motivations and reasons for ending the tobacco habit.
5. During the evening, or at any other more convenient time of day, hypnotize yourself and play the recording of suggestions on quitting. If you have been unable to record this, have someone read it to you.
6. Add any other of your own suggestions.

Second day

1. Double the number of cigarettes smoked. Be sure you smoke them all.
2. Read over your motivations again.
3. Use self-hypnosis.
4. Listen to recorded suggestions and add your own.

Third day

Use the same procedure as on the second day. On going to bed that night, throw away any extra left-over cigarettes. Keep on with double the number of cigarettes usually smoked.

E-day

Now you have stopped smoking as of the night before, when you went to sleep. You are an ex-smoker. Think of yourself in this way.

1. After breakfast brush your teeth and use a mouthwash.
2. At each meal chew your food longer.
3. Use lozenges whenever you want to do so.
4. Counteract any thought or desire about smoking immediately when one comes to mind. Use the Yoga breathing exercise. Then distract your mind or busy yourself doing something.
5. Immediately after breakfast read over your list of motivations.
6. During the evening, or when most convenient, use self-hypnosis and listen to recorded suggestions. Add any others of your own.
7. While in hypnosis use visual imagery of yourself

as a non-smoker in scenes where others are smoking.

Repeat this program for the next two days. Then begin omitting whatever of these activities that seem unimportant or no longer needed. Continue counteracting any desire to smoke that pops up. During the next few days occasionally use self-hypnosis and listen to the recorded suggestions. Frequency as to this will depend on the ease you find in ending the habit.

Daily program for the addict or heavy smoker.

It is important to omit nothing in this schedule and to adhere to it as given.

First day—with E-day set-up as five days later

1. Buy all the supplies you will need, gum, lozenges, imitation cigarettes, fruit juices, mouthwash, lobeline sulphate in lozenge form (it comes in various brand names—ask your druggist), and a tranquilizer as prescribed by your doctor.
2. Start taking your tranquilizer according to the directions given you by your physician.
3. Tell all your friends and acquaintances that you will stop smoking on your E-day.
4. Change the brand of cigarettes you smoke.
5. Write out your list of motivations and reasons why you want to stop smoking. Use the list given in the text and add any personal ones of your own.
6. Use self-hypnosis, selecting a time of day best suited for you. Probably after dinner in the evening would be best, or on going to bed.

7. Play your recorded suggestions, or have them read to you.
8. Add any other suggestions of your own.
9. Use visual imagery, seeing yourself in situations where you previously would have smoked, but are not now smoking. See yourself being offered a cigarette and refusing it.

Second and third days

1. Take tranquilizers as directed.
2. Read over your motivations.
3. Use self-hypnosis.
4. Listen to recorded suggestions, add your own suggestions.
5. Use more visual imagery.

Fourth and fifth days

Follow the same schedule but increase the number of cigarettes smoked. If your average was two packs a day or less, double the number to be smoked. If more than two packs, smoke an additional two packs. Be sure all your excess quota is smoked. When ready to go to sleep the night of the fifth day, throw away any left-over cigarettes.

E-day and the following two days

1. Drink a glass of juice immediately on awakening, before dressing.
2. Brush teeth before dressing.
3. Immediately after breakfast brush teeth, use mouthwash.
4. Take tranquilizers as directed.
5. Take lobeline sulphate tablet after each meal.

6. Use gum, lozenges, or other "crutches" as you feel the need.
7. Chew all food longer at meals.
8. Immediately counteract any thought of smoking with counterthoughts, distracting mind, 4-8-4 breathing exercise, and follow with some activity.
9. At the most convenient time, probably during the evening, read over your list of motives.
10. Use self-hypnosis.
11. Listen to recorded suggestions, adding any individual ones.
12. Use visual imagery.

Continue with this program each day for the next two weeks, though you can moderate the use of steps 9, 10, 11, and 12. Do not eliminate these steps but use them occasionally when you think them needed. Your program in this way will depend very largely on how easy you find it to continue your non-smoking. Most readers will have very little difficulty even on E-day, and will find each day still easier. After the first week there may be some desire to smoke but it can easily be dismissed as soon as it arises.

Summary

With E-day you have definite procedures to follow, as well as taking certain steps for a few days before E-day. Detailed daily programs are given for the light and medium smoker, and for the heavy or addicted smoker.

The main techniques in your program of quitting are to counter any urge to smoke that arises, using a counter-suggestion, diverting your mind, taking up some other activity, and using the 4-8-4 breathing exercise. You will frequently use self-hypnosis and listen to the recorded suggestions.

You do not have to gain weight when you have stopped smoking. Awareness of the possibility, with suggestions to counteract it, chewing your food longer, all these things will serve to prevent gaining weight.

About three months after you've stopped smoking, and again at the end of about a year, there is a danger. This is the thought as to what smoking a cigarette would be like. Yielding to this temptation is almost certain to start you off as a smoker again.

After being a heavy smoker for many years, the author applied the methods given in this book and quit smoking with ease, although he had previously been unable to stop. You, too, should have little or no difficulty.

13

Recorded Suggestions to Help You Stop Smoking

You will be playing over or listening to someone read these suggestions to you frequently during the days just before your E-day, when you actually stop smoking. You also will want to play them occasionally after E-day. These ideas and thoughts are worded, of course, to apply to any reader of this book, either male. or female, either a light smoker or a real cigarette addict. In making a recording, or in having someone read the words to you, they can be changed a bit to fit your own particular situation. Some parts may be omitted, if you feel that they don't apply to you. You can substitute other wording that might better fit your case. Read the chapter carefully. Then go back over it, noting any changes you wish to make, adding such other suggestions as could be helpful.

Remember how often TV commercials are repeated? They are suggestions, rubbed into your subconscious by repetition. Repetition is one of the main ways of making suggestions most effective. So you should play over these recorded suggestions a number of times, or have them read to you several times. (I'll only mention recording in future, it being understood that these suggestions will be read if you cannot record them.)

When you've decided on your E-day, start playing the recording at least once each day. You'll need to play it possibly after you have quit smoking, though your program may go so well that this won't be needed.

After you have made a recording and are ready to begin listening to the wording, you should have your tape recorder or record player already adjusted and ready to play. You should be in a position so you need only to reach over and turn it on after you've hypnotized yourself. Then you can settle back, relax still more and listen attentively. When the recording has been played, you can then shut it off.

Here is the wording to be recorded.

"Now that you have put yourself into hypnosis, you can be receptive to some ideas and suggestions which will help you end the cigarette habit with little or no difficulty. As you listen to my voice let yourself drift a little deeper now. Just drift deeper with each breath you take. You've found how pleasant it is to relax so completely, to let yourself drift off in this way. The deeper you go, the more pleasant and comfortable it is, so relax now. Relax now still more. Drift still deeper while you listen. You can shut out all outside sounds. They are not important; just center your attention on what I am saying. Nothing else seems important now, while you are listening. Drift deeper and concentrate on the words you'll be hearing.

"These suggestions are intended to help you. They are all for your benefit. No one is making you stop smoking.

You could double the number of cigarettes you smoke if you wanted to do so. But of course you don't want to do that. Instead you want to quit smoking.

"Some people feel resentful and become irritable when they quit smoking. This is because they really don't want to quit but think they should. They resent going through the quitting process. Because they don't really want to quit, it is very hard to stop and they think a great deal about smoking; with strong desire to smoke. Probably there are withdrawal symptoms. This brings resentment and irritability. Since you really want to stop and no one is forcing you to do it, you'll be free of any feelings of resentment. Instead you'll be glad you have finally made up your mind to stop. There will be no tendency to be irritable or cross. Irritability is usually taken out on your family—those around you. Instead of being irritable, you'll be relieved and glad that you are no longer a slave to a weed, for that is what tobacco is, just a weed.

"In the past when you first learned to smoke, you began with the wish to be "one of the gang," to do as your friends and others of your age were doing. You wanted to be grown up, an adult. Smoking seemed to you to be a sign of adulthood.

"Now that you *are* adult, really adult, you view smoking in a different way. You don't have to prove to your friends that you are adult. Now you don't have to prove how mature you are. You don't need to smoke to show that you're manly or womanly. As you see it now, you were really immature when you began to smoke instead of being mature.

"You've smoked because it seemed to give you satisfaction in one way or another. But has it really been so satisfactory? Do you really enjoy the taste of tobacco? I'll bet you don't. Do you enjoy the smell of tobacco smoke? I doubt it. When you really think about it, there's nothing pleasant at all about smoking, and very many things about it are unpleasant.

"Did you ever get smoke in your eyes? Of course you have sometimes when you were smoking. Remember how it smarted and how the tears came? Do you remember coming into a room where many people were smoking and how your eyes soon began to smart? That's the stuff you've been inhaling and drawing down into your lungs. It's affected the lung tissue much as it has affected your eyes. If it irritates your eyes so much when a tiny amount of smoke touches the eyeballs, what an effect it must have on your bronchial tubes and lung tissue, for they are almost as sensitive as is the tissue of the eyeball. One obvious result of this irritation is your tendency to cough and the secretion of additional phlegm to protect the tissue.

"Whenever you accomplish something it promotes a feeling of satisfaction. If it's something hard to do, then there's a greater sense of satisfaction in accomplishment. In stopping smoking you'll have great satisfaction in being successful. And you will be successful. You'll have much more satisfaction in stopping smoking than you've had in the past from smoking. It's a real accomplishment to stop, of which you can be proud, even though you'll undoubtedly find that it is surprisingly easy for you to quit.

"There really is nothing good about cigarettes. They neither taste nor smell good. They may have seemed to quiet your nerves when you smoked them. But within a short time after you finished a cigarette, you developed even more nervousness. Tobacco isn't a sedative. It's a stimulant. If you are listening to this recording before your

E-day and have not yet stopped smoking, notice how soon after finishing one cigarette you begin to feel nervous tension.

"On the last two days before your E-day, when you've increased the number of cigarettes you smoke, notice particularly that this excessive smoking makes you more nervous. It will really be a great relief not to have to smoke any more. About six days after you have quit, with the nicotine all out of your system, you'll undoubtedly find you are less nervous and are more relaxed and free of tension than you've been in a long time.

"Perhaps you've been approaching your E-day with a little apprehension, afraid you may have a hard time quitting. It is rather natural to have some doubts but, as you come nearer and nearer to E-day and actually quitting, you'll find yourself eager to be free of this annoying smoking habit. You'll become more and more sure that you'll be rid of the habit with relative ease. Each time you listen to these ideas you will become more and more sure you can do it. You'll become more convinced that you can quit without difficulty. You'll be more and more determined to become an ex-smoker and will never smoke again.

"If you've tried to stop smoking before, you may have had withdrawal symptoms and found it so unpleasant that you couldn't quit. Probably you found you were continually thinking of how you wanted a cigarette. Realize that you now are approaching this problem in an entirely different way, with tools and techniques which have helped many others stop successfully and easily.

"Now you can use hypnosis. You'll have the help and be aided by your subconscious mind. It will be working for you and helping you. You are bound to have some thoughts of smoking and some mild desire to smoke, but you'll easily cope with this and your inner mind will keep such thoughts and wishes to a minimum so they seldom come to you. That part of your mind will understand and realize that smoking is bad for you, is detrimental to you in every way.

"You have decided to stop smoking. There are many reasons why you've come to such a decision. Let's review them so that your inner mind fully appreciates all these bad aspects of smoking. Of course the first and primary motive for you to stop is for health. You know that exhaustive investigation has shown that cigarette smoking can and does cause lung cancer. Other types of smoking, pipe and cigars, sometimes cause lip cancer. You know that respiratory illnesses such as bronchitis and emphysema often result from smoking. Perhaps you would not be a victim of these diseases, but it is a definite possibility that you might be. You would not willingly expose yourself to some infectious disease. And now you will no longer risk the possibility of getting some disease as a result of smoking.

"If you have children, you do not want them to run the risk of having any of these diseases. You now know all the disadvantages of smoking and if you could live your life over would never have started to smoke, having your present knowledge about it. So you don't want your children to smoke, if you have any children. If a parent smokes, the children almost always follow the example set by the parent and begin to smoke at an early age. So you will not want to set such an example.

"Smoking is expensive. If you smoked only one pack of cigarettes a day for forty years it would cost you about $4000 plus probably as much more for ashtrays, matches, cigarette lighters, cleaning clothes, burns, and other expenses. And what you have done is actually burned up all that money. It certainly seems silly when you think about it. Now you are going to save all the money you would otherwise burn up and waste.

"It will be a relief to you to know that you no longer smell of tobacco, that your breath is fresh instead of foul, that your clothes are clean and free of ashes and odors, your fingers unstained, and your teeth whiter.

"You'll realize all the other reasons and motives for stopping smoking, to sleep better, feel better, enjoy foods because they taste better, to have less nervous tension and other reasons which will apply particularly to yourself.

"When you stop smoking food does taste better, but that doesn't mean you need eat more. Some people have a tendency to overeat when they quit smoking, but you are aware of this and will be careful to eat properly. You will eat only enough to give you the amount of energy you need. You will watch to see that you do not eat more than you did before stopping smoking. Your appetite will be fully satisfied with an amount of food just sufficient to keep you in good health and with the energy you need. You will maintain your weight at the proper level for your body.

"If a thought of smoking, a desire for a cigarette comes into your mind, you will recognize it as a danger signal. You will get rid of the idea immediately by counteracting it. You will think, "I don't need to smoke." You'll at once go through one cycle of your breathing exercise. Then distract your mind with some activity, either mental or physical. After E-day these thoughts will come to you less and less frequently with each passing day. You may find that you do not have them at all, that you have stopped smoking and definitely do not *want* to smoke.

"On your E-day you'll awaken glad you do not have to smoke as you did for the past two days. You'll drink some fruit juice at once and brush your teeth, repeating this after your breakfast and using a mouthwash when you've brushed them. You will feel relieved that the day has finally come when you have become an ex-smoker. Do not think of yourself as in the process of quitting. That keeps it in the present. You *have* quit. Now you are an ex-smoker. Smoking is something in your past, that you're glad to have ended. You are now through with the nasty habit.

"Others at times will be smoking around you, perhaps members of your family, or friends, or even strangers. Smelling their tobacco smoke will not affect you in any way. It will not be unpleasant enough to bother you but it will not smell good to you, rather it will be almost neutral. You'll pay no attention to tobacco smoke.

"Watching others smoke will give you a feeling of superiority and accomplishment. You can feel that these people are foolish to smoke, but that it's their business, not yours. You feel a bit sorry for them that they have not been smart enough to stop as you have done.

"Quitting smoking is not a matter of will-power. It is determination, not will power, that is important. Determination plus a real desire to be completely rid of the smoking habit makes it easy to quit. Self-hypnosis and your own suggestions can add power to both your desire and your determination. You are determined to end the habit, determined not even to want to smoke. You are stronger than any habit, once you want to break a habit. You *want* to stop smoking. You are going to stop on your

E-day; if you are listening to these words after E-day, you have already stopped smoking. With E-day your desire to remain stopped, and your determination to win and overcome this habit grows stronger with each day that passes.

"Now drift a little deeper into hypnosis. Drift deeper and relax even more. Using your imagination, visualize yourself in a social crowd of your friends. There are several people of both sexes in the group. You are sitting in the midst of the group in a comfortable chair, or perhaps on a couch, exchanging talk with some of the others, smiling and perfectly at ease. Some of the others are smoking. You can see cigarettes in their hands or in their mouths as they draw on them. See someone offer you a cigarette. But you shake your head in refusal. You are smiling and saying that you do not smoke.

"Now change the scene. Form a visual image of a business group of some kind, whatever kind of business meeting you might be attending. See yourself in this group, with others there smoking. Some are talking to you and someone offers you a cigarette, holding out a package to you. Again you shake your head in refusal and you tell the others that you do not smoke. Imagine those nearest you telling you how wise you are, commending and congratulating you.

"No one is making you stop smoking. You are quitting or have stopped because that is what you want, because you are intelligent and sensible and it is the intelligent, wise thing to do to rid yourself of the tobacco habit. You will feel no resentment and will feel mellow and happy at being able to stop. You'll feel very contented and happy all through the period of breaking off the habit. You will enjoy yourself all through this period.

"You will remember to carry out all the suggestions and ideas which have been given in your book which will help you end the habit easily. Your determination and desire to end the habit are increasing each day. Having stopped, they become still stronger. The thought of smoking becomes distasteful. The thought of the taste and smell of tobacco seems unpleasant. Following E-day, you know you'll never smoke again. What a relief it will be not to need or have any desire to smoke. Following E-day you are through, will never smoke again.

"Your inner mind is to help you in every way possible to be free of the desire to smoke, to be free of thoughts about smoking. You will find it quite easy to end the habit and within a short time after stopping you will be feeling much healthier, sleeping better, finding your sense of smell and taste improved, having less nervous tension, with your mind functioning more clearly and logically. You no longer want to smoke. You are or soon will be completely free of the tobacco habit.

"Now you have been very nicely relaxed and comfortable. As you practice self-hypnosis you'll be able to reach a good depth and your inner mind is to carry out any suggestion which you give yourself that would be of benefit to you.

"You'll now be able to carry out your program of stopping smoking. You can quickly be rid of the desire to smoke and able to be completely rid of the tobacco habit.

"Now you can awaken yourself at your leisure. You can awaken as you wish. Just count to three with the thought that you are going to awaken and you will be wide awake."

14

How to Cut Down
Your Smoking

What if you fail to stop smoking?

A few who use these methods will fail in their effort
to eliminate the tobacco habit. I want to give this consideration for there is no way of stopping smoking which
would be infallible. When this happens, there is a reason
for failure. If, unfortunately, you should be one of the few
who are not successful, perhaps you'll make it with further effort, if you can locate the reason for failure.

Your mental attitude is the most probable cause of failure to stop smoking. Perhaps you were not able to gen-
erate a really strong desire to stop, and only felt that you
should quit. If you had strong doubts of your ability to
lick the habit, this may have entered in. By reading over
again the main reasons why you should quit, and with
more hypnotic suggestions aimed at instilling confidence
rather than doubts in your mind, you may be able to overcome these possible reasons for failure.

Why you can't stop.

There may be psychological reasons for your lack of success. Sometimes an idea will become fixed in the subconscious part of the mind, acting then like a post-hypnotic suggestion. Some ideas can set up a mental block preventing success. These fixed ideas usually are formed at a time when you are under some emotion. Probably you then have slipped spontaneously into hypnosis and are very suggestible.

Suppose, as an example, that you had tried to stop smoking and were angry at yourself when you had failed —this being a previous attempt to stop. Someone might have planted an idea by making some such remark as, "Well, you're hooked. You never will be able to stop smoking." This same idea could be worded in various other ways. Becoming a fixed idea, it would make it impossible for you to stop smoking, until such an idea was removed. Hypnotic suggestion could counteract it and remove it.

Almost everyone at times develops a need for self-punishment. Technically it's called *masochism*. You probably are not wearing a halo. Everyone does things he shouldn't, which are regretted. Guilt feelings are likely to call for self-punishment. Psychotherapists are well aware that masochism may even lead to self-destruction. There is no doubt that cigarette smoking carried to excess sometimes is masochistic even to the point of being self-destructive. Of course this may not be true in your case. It is only one of several possibilities that caused you to fail in your effort to stop smoking.

The only contraindication for stopping smoking is if a

person is extremely nervous, agitated and depressed. If you are under such tension that you are verging on a nervous breakdown, or so emotionally disturbed that you might be about to "go off your rocker," then you certainly should not make an attempt to stop smoking. It could be much the lesser of two evils.

A young woman in her early thirties came to me saying she wanted to stop smoking but had found she couldn't. Her doctor had told her she had stomach ulcers and should stop smoking. At his instruction she was now dieting. Would I help her with hypnosis?

Ruth, we will call her, seemed a bit nervous but was a fairly good hypnotic subject. She did not want to go through any preparatory exercises—she wanted to stop right that day. She was given suggestions which could help her, but they were made permissively, not as commands. She was told to return two days later.

When she arrived, I found her extremely agitated. She was nervous and jittery, and told me she had not been asleep since I had seen her. Instead of her usual two packs a day she had been smoking four, although she had tried not to smoke at all. She seemed to be on the verge of a psychotic break. I told her there was some unconscious reason for this condition and that she should not attempt to stop smoking. After hypnotizing her again, she was given suggestions removing all that I had made before, and told to continue smoking at least for the time being.

After awakening the girl, I told her that she definitely should have treatment to learn the reasons for this situation and until then should continue to smoke, even though it was physically bad for her. She refused to consider psychotherapy, but had now calmed down. I did not see her again. This is the only case in my personal experience where quitting smoking was definitely inadvisable. With psychotherapy she might later have been able safely to stop smoking.

If you found you could not stop entirely, try to keep the number of cigarettes smoked to a minimum—in other words cut down. See if you can form a group of friends who wish to quit smoking. You may have much better results working in a group, particularly when you have reread all the good reasons for ending the habit. Then perhaps your mental attitude will be different so that you can be successful and stop.

How you can cut down in your smoking.

Undoubtedly some who read this book will not want to stop smoking. Probably such a person would admit that he would be better off to stop but he lacks incentive. He enjoys smoking, feels a great satisfaction from it and feels that the chances of his developing any illness from smoking are very remote. If he has smoked for a number of years, he is likely to think that any such condition would have already been present if it were ever to affect him.

Such a person probably would be one who smokes at least a pack a day and probably more and probably will think it wise to cut down in the number of cigarettes smoked but not to stop altogether. Is it possible to cut down and keep your smoking to a less quantity?

I am sure that this can be done but on the other hand there will be some who try to cut down who will be again smoking as much as before after a short time. I don't want to be discouraging about this. You may well find yourself able to maintain the lesser number smoked. For some time you will need to keep your program active to avoid the possibility of gradually increasing the quantity. You should carefully keep track of the number of cigarettes smoked for three or four months after starting to cut down.

A program for cutting down.

In order to reduce your smoking, you'll be breaking up an old habit pattern. However it will be much easier to do this than to stop entirely. Your program will be somewhat similar to that advocated for quitting, but modified and requiring less time and effort. You'll find self-hypnosis the most valuable help for your purpose.

After having learned self-hypnosis, set the day for the start of your cutting down program. Instead of the five day period prior to quitting, make it only three days, as you will not be going through as many preliminaries. At least once a day on these three days put yourself in hypnosis and listen to the recorded suggestions on lessening the amount of your smoking. These are given in the next chapter, following the recording of suggestions intended for those who plan to quit smoking entirely. While in hypnosis add any of your own suggestions to the recorded ones.

You do not need to use any of the aids recommended for quitting smoking, drugs, lozenges, etc. However, do prepare a list of reasons why you wish to cut down on the amount of your smoking. Read this over each day, the three preliminary ones and the next three days after you start to cut down.

To what extent do you wish to cut down? Probably most smokers who wish to follow this policy will aim at restricting their consumption to about half the number being smoked. Let us say you have been smoking two packs a day and wish to cut it to only one, from forty to twenty a day. For the first week set your quota at thirty instead of forty. This certainly will not be hard to do, and it is better not to attempt too much at first. You can apportion the thirty as you wish but be sure you have only that number available for the day. Space your smoking so you do not run out before late evening.

After you have reduced your quota to thirty and continued this for a week, set it at twenty-five for a four-day period. Then you are all set to go to twenty.

During the three day preliminary period you would find it helpful later if you would note the exact time each time you smoke. Keep a piece of paper on which you can note this down, and make it a point to notice the hour and record it for each cigarette. Probably you'll note the cycle I've mentioned, though emotions and changes in your daily routine would influence this.

From this record of your smoking you can ration yourself better each time you cut the number to be smoked. You may be smoking more or less than two packs a day, and this number has only been used to show how, in general, you should plan your cutting down. For other quantities make it somewhat proportionate. If you should be a real addict smoking perhaps four packs a day, cut first to three, then to two, and finally to one, if that is your eventual goal.

How to stay at a reduced quantity.

For many who wish only to cut down rather than quit smoking, your difficulty will be to stay at the less quantity. You may have to keep close track of your consumption for two, three, or even four months. You are breaking up one habit and substituting another, as to frequency of smoking. The new one must be well established or you are likely to creep up gradually to the former habit and be back where you were. Being aware of the likelihood, you should be able to avoid it. I would recommend that you buy your cigarettes by the carton and keep track of the date of each purchase. You can then readily note if your consumption begins to increase, and check it at once.

While it may be something of a nuisance to keep some of these records, without them you'll be unable to know whether you are reaching your goal and maintaining it. The tendency will be to rationalize that you are, but actually to slip back gradually to the former number of cigarettes smoked. If it is worthwhile for you to reduce your smoking, it should not be too much trouble to keep these simple records.

Many readers who conscientiously and determinedly work to cut down will be successful and will continue to smoke the lesser quantity. For those who may fail and who find themselves returning to excessive smoking, probably the best plan would be to try turning to pipe or cigar smoking. This might be the answer for the person who definitely does not wish to stop smoking entirely.

Your daily program for cutting down.

As with the person who wishes to stop smoking, it is best to start cutting down at some time where your usual daily routine is interrupted, as when on a trip. Otherwise select a weekend to initiate your plan. This would mean cutting down first on Saturday. Three days before, on Wednesday, would be the beginning of your program.

First day

In a notebook or on a sheet of paper note down the exact time of day whenever you smoke. Make no attempt to cut the number of cigarettes smoked. Follow this procedure for the three day period. This will give you the usual pattern which you have been following and any cycle that may be present.

1. In the evening or at any convenient time use self-hypnosis and listen to your recorded suggestions. Add any of your own.
2. Make a list of all the reasons why you have decided to reduce or cut down on your smoking.
3. Make a decision as to your goal—what quota you are setting yourself as to the number you will smoke.

Second and third day

Keep track of your smoking. In the evening use self-hypnosis and play your recording. Read over your motives.

Fourth day

This is the day when you start to cut down. For this and the next two days smoke approximately one-fourth less than you have been smoking. Ration yourself somewhat as follows. If you formerly smoked 40 cigarettes, you'll smoke 30 now. Set your quota for ten in the morning, ten in the afternoon, and eight in the evening. This leaves two as leeway which can be smoked as need arises. Whatever has been your past quantity, set your quota similarly, allowing two or three extra to be smoked as desired.

Use self-hypnosis and your recording. Read over your motivations again.

After the fourth day

Your main job is to watch carefully as to the number of cigarettes smoked, keeping strictly to your quota. Use self-hypnosis and listen to your recording two or three times during the next week.

On the fourth day cut your quota to one-half of the original number smoked. If your aim is to cut down still further, plan to make the further reduction five days later.

Each day make it a point to carry with you only your quota for the day, otherwise you will likely exceed the number you have allowed yourself.

When you have reduced your quota to that which you want to maintain, for three days keep a record again of the time of day when each cigarette is smoked, comparing this record with the former one you made.

SUMMARY

A few who try to stop smoking with these methods may fail. If so there is some reason for lack of success. It may be your mental attitude with doubts of success, or you may not have decided definitely that you really want to quit. Perhaps some other psychological reason may be present. Some smokers are unconsciously being self-destructive.

Contraindications as to stopping smoking would be the extremely disturbed person, one who is badly depressed, or one on the verge of a nervous or mental breakdown. In these situations it would be inadvisable to stop smoking until the condition is overcome. If some illness makes it essential to stop smoking, psychotherapeutic treatment is indicated.

Some readers will prefer to cut down on the quantity smoked rather than to stop entirely. The tendency for most who attempt to restrict but not end their smoking is to return gradually to the number formerly smoked, to cut down only temporarily. By using determination and watching carefully so as not to exceed the new quota, many will be able to remain at the lesser number smoked, setting up a new habit pattern.

If there is failure and a return to excessive smoking, it might be well to turn to pipe or cigar smoking, if it is decided to keep on using tobacco.

15

Recorded Suggestions to Use
in Cutting Down

Those who have made a decision to cut down on the number of cigarettes smoked rather than to stop smoking will find the suggestions for recording given here of help in their program. The situation is entirely different here than for those wishing to quit entirely. In quitting the aim is to remove desire for a smoke. Here we want only to space out the time between cigarettes so that at the end of the day a less quantity has been used.

In making a record of when you have smoked, of the time at which each cigarette was smoked, you undoubtedly can see a pattern. Probably you have smoked from one to three cigarettes before breakfast, one immediately after each meal, one as an accompaniment to a cup of coffee or drink such as a cocktail. In between these cigarettes you have probably found a certain time lapse. Every so often you reached for a cigarette. This time lapse was probably regular except that it would be influenced by changes in your day's activities and routine. If seated at your desk there would be a certain period between cigarettes. If driving a car, about the same lapsed periods would occur. For the housewife it would be similar. Even slight emotional upsets, minor irritations, anything going a bit wrong, would call for a cigarette and break the more usual pattern.

In becoming a more moderate smoker it is these patterns we expect to change, principally to make the more routine spacing between cigarettes longer. You would not be very successful if you tried to eliminate those cigarettes which give the most satisfaction and are the more pleasurable ones—such as the ones immediately after a meal. It is much easier to cut out those which give much less satisfaction. These are almost invariably the cigarettes smoked late in the morning, during the latter part of the afternoon, and late in the evening.

You will undoubtedly find that cutting your smoking to a much less number each day will lead to more satisfaction in those you do smoke. It is this fact that will make it easier for you to cut down. You'll only be eliminating the ones which have not tasted good and which you've smoked largely as a matter of habit rather than because you wanted one at the time.

I've recommended a change of brand preliminary to stopping smoking. This will not apply for the person wishing to cut down, because he would find the new brand not satisfying his desire or his taste and he would probably increase the number smoked in an effort to satisfy this desire. So, if you plan on cutting down, continue with your regular brand during the preliminary period and as you follow the reduced program.

In setting up a quota for morning, afternoon, and evening, try to eliminate the cigarettes which would be of least importance and least satisfying. If you have normally smoked three before breakfast, it will be easy to eliminate one, and perhaps two. Longer spacing between smokes eliminates several others, and you will find other times and situations where it is easy to cut the number smoked. This of course will vary a great deal in individuals. The routine of a housewife is entirely different from that of an actress; that of a businessman completely dissimilar to that of a truckdriver.

Your suggestions for recording.

"You have now let yourself drift into hypnosis and are all relaxed and comfortable. Drift still deeper as you listen to my voice. Let yourself relax still more. Go deeper with each breath you take. Drift deeper. The deeper in hypnosis you are, the more comfortable and pleasant you find it.

"As you listen, shut out any outside sounds that might be disturbing. They can go in one ear and out the other. Pay attention only to my voice. Nothing else is important. Drift deeper and concentrate on what I'm saying. Every suggestion I will make, every idea stated here, is for your benefit and is intended to help you. Your inner mind should realize this and accept these thoughts and carry them out, helping you realize your goal.

"You have decided that it would be wise and beneficial for you to cut down somewhat on your smoking. You do not wish to stop smoking, but think that modifying the number smoked would be best for you. You have made this decision for various good reasons. You have recognized that excessive smoking can be damaging to your health when continued over a long period. Of course you want to retain your health, not to suffer from any of the illnesses which can be caused by excessive smoking.

"You have other motives for cutting down on your smoking. You will be saving money, you will be accomplishing something, and you'll take pride in accomplishing it. Anyone gets a feeling of satisfaction from accomplishment. And you have still other reasons why it is best for you to cut the number of cigarettes you'll be smoking.

"No one is making you do this. You could, instead of reducing the quantity you smoke, increase it to double the number. That is not what you want, and would be foolish. You want to reduce the number so that you are smoking moderately. With no compulsion to do this, of course you will not feel irritable in cutting down. You can even feel a relief at ridding yourself of excessive smoking which could be harmful to you.

"You'll feel very glad that you've reached a sensible decision to cut down on your smoking. You have developed a habit pattern in your smoking which you have been following. Now you are merely going to change this pattern somewhat. You will not be feeling deprived because you will be smoking all that you really want to smoke. The cigarettes you'll be eliminating will be the ones which were excess, which really did not taste good or satisfy you, and which actually were unnecessary to your needs and desires about smoking. You'll continue to smoke the ones you really enjoy, and to smoke at the times when you've enjoyed smoking. So you'll not be depriving yourself of any enjoyment. Instead you'll be benefiting yourself.

"You will be making a note of the pattern of your daily smoking, or you may already have listed the times you've smoked. There has been something of a cycle in it, and you are merely going to extend that cycle a little. If you have tended to take about a half hour between cigarettes during your daily routine, you'll now be taking just a little longer, about forty-five minutes instead. If you've been taking an hour between smokes on the average, now it will be about eighty minutes instead of sixty. Whatever the cyclic time has been, your subconscious mind will now extend it about fifty percent or thereabouts. It will do this routinely, extending the average time between cigarettes. At first you will do this consciously, actually timing yourself. Soon your inner mind will take this over and see that your time between smokes is extended so that you do not even think about it consciously. You'll be setting up a new habit pattern as to this.

"You wish to keep your smoking to a moderate number of cigarettes daily. You want this to become a permanent pattern, a new habit replacing the old one which was detrimental because you were smoking too much. You will be perfectly satisfied with the new pattern because the cigarettes you are eliminating are the ones which were least satisfying and were not really needed.

"In breaking up the old habit you will often find the thought of smoking coming to mind according to that old routine, sooner than it will with the new pattern. You can readily counter the wish for a smoke at that time by merely thinking to yourself, 'It isn't time yet. I don't need a smoke now until a little later.' Then you'll find the desire to smoke has disappeared and you can wait to smoke until the time you have set as your new quota.

"In setting your quota for morning, afternoon, and evening, you have a little leeway, two or three cigarettes left over or not assigned. This gives you a feeling of confidence, a feeling that you have cigarettes available if

changes in your routine are such that you have a strong
desire to smoke at some certain time or more often than
your quota has scheduled. Often, though, your day will
go so smoothly that you'll end up not having smoked your
reserve.

"Your inner mind is to help you in your program of cutting down in every way possible, keeping the desire to
smoke at a minimum, spacing the time longer between
cigarettes, and keeping nervous tension at a minimum.

"If you have smoked so much that you've been bothered by hacking and coughing when you wake up in
the morning, reducing the quantity smoked will probably
relieve this so that you need not cough on awakening, so
that your mouth tastes fresh instead of sour and unpleasant.

"Having made up your mind that it is best to reduce
the number of cigarettes you will be smoking, it will be
easy for you to carry this out just as you have planned.
You will follow the quota you have set and will find that
it is easy to follow. You are really eliminating only excess
cigarettes, the ones which were really not needed and
which gave you little or no satisfaction. You will not miss
them. You will enjoy the ones you do smoke even more
because you have cut out the ones which made your
mouth taste bad due to smoking too much.

"You will quickly set up a new pattern of smoking with
the eliminating of certain times when you smoked and by
extending the length of time between cigarettes. Within
a short time, probably only two or three weeks, this new
pattern will have become a habit which will have replaced
the old one and you will then maintain it, keeping to the
reduced quota you have set yourself. Soon you will no
longer need to think about keeping to this quota but

your subconscious mind will take over and see that you maintain it.

"With each day that passes during this period of cutting down, it will be easier and easier for you to keep to your quota, to find that you are smoking all that you want to smoke and that it is easy to postpone any desire to smoke that arises until your new pattern has become an established habit.

"You have been nicely relaxed and comfortable as you have listened. When you practice self-hypnosis you'll be able to reach a good depth and your inner mind is to carry out any suggestion you may give yourself that would be of benefit to you.

"You will easily carry out your program of cutting down on your smoking and will quickly have made it permanent.

"Now you can awaken yourself at your leisure, whenever you wish to do so. Just count to three with the thought that you are going to awaken and you will be wide awake."

The report of the Surgeon General's Committee has mentioned that almost everyone who begins to smoke will find himself smoking some certain amount which changes only slightly from day to day. This quantity quota seems to become established within two or three years after smoking is begun. A different pattern is seen here to narcotic addiction where there is a continually increasing need for more of the drug to satisfy the craving. With cigarette smoking if the pattern is one pack a day it remains so over the years, remains at whatever has become the need pattern.

In cutting down you are going to upset this pattern and quite naturally it will take some time to establish a new one which will be permanent. Even after three or four months there may be some tendency to drift back toward the old pattern. If you are aware of this, and watch carefully that you maintain the new quota, you can continue it indefinitely. You should check periodically, however, to see that you are not going over this quota.

16

How to Reach the Big Decision

It has not been intended for this book to be a sermon on the evils of smoking. I have rather wanted to give you all the real facts about cigarette smoking in particular, and how it can affect your health. What you do about it is then up to you. If you should decide to stop smoking, a relatively easy way of doing so has been given. In case you prefer to cut down in the amount of your smoking, you are shown how this can be accomplished. When you have completed the book, you should be able to decide what procedure you wish to follow.

Together with other reports, the Surgeon General's statement as to the effect of tobacco on health has made many smokers give consideration to the situation they are in. These reports have aroused fear but fear is not enough deterrent to lead most smokers to stop. The person who finds great satisfaction in smoking is going to be very reluctant to give up the habit. He has no desire to stop, nor probably any intention of trying to break off. This probably applies to the great majority of smokers.

They will continue to smoke and will not reduce the volume of cigarettes consumed.

A person in this category might theoretically like to cut down a little, but he is not willing to make any effort to curtail his smoking. He'll keep the pattern he has set up. He'll shrug off any passing thought about quitting or cutting down. He has accepted himself as a smoker and ignores possible health hazards.

The only thing that would ever cause him to make any effort to stop would be if he should develop some illness, such for example as Buerger's disease, where it is imperative for him to stop smoking. Even then, this type of smoker will probably have great difficulty controlling his smoking habit because he doesn't want to stop. Most such smokers will never have to face this situation, but it will develop for some of them.

A large percentage of cigarette smokers undoubtedly wish they had never begun to smoke. They would not have started if they could have known then what they know now. These people would be glad to stop now if all desire for cigarettes could be made to disappear with a snap of the fingers or a wave of a magic wand.

This type of smoker is likely to be very doubtful of being able to quit smoking. Perhaps he has tried previously, has had strong withdrawal symptoms and a bad time, with resultant failure to stop. This makes for reluctance to try again. Is it worthwhile to go through all that again and probably fail again?

The smoker who has no intention of trying to stop smoking is not likely to have taken the time to read this book. If you have read this far, undoubtedly you have had thoughts of quitting. Now you'll be faced with making a decision. Should you accept your fate as being a confirmed smoker who can't break off, or should you try the methods advocated here?

The person who smokes only lightly, or would be classed as a medium smoker will probably find it easy to reach a decision. He will not have all the doubts of the heavier smoker. He may think his smoking is not enough to make him very susceptible to the illnesses which he now recognizes can be caused by cigarette smoking, and therefore it is not important for him to quit. If he finds much satisfaction from his smoking, he may decide to continue, perhaps wish to cut down a bit.

The wiser person will feel that it is not worthwhile to take any chance with his health and will make the decision to stop smoking. It will be easy for him to follow the program given which applies best to him. He will be successful and will be most unlikely ever to return to smoking at a later date. He'll be a permanent ex-smoker.

It is the heavy smoker and the addict who will find it most difficult to make a decision about quitting or continuing to smoke, or cutting down. Yet it is this kind of smoker who is most likely to incur the diseases caused by smoking, for they have much the greatest incidence in heavy smokers. So healthwise it is more important for such a smoker to decide to stop.

My advice to this type of smoker is to forget past experiences where he may have failed in attempting to quit. You've been given the "secret formula." It's a very simple one. If you really want to stop, if you can say to yourself, "I'm through. I've had enough. My health is too important to me and I don't have to be a slave to this infernal weed any longer," then you've reached the place where you can quit with relative ease. I was in the addict class and I found it easy when I applied these methods. I can't emphasize enough that the desire to stop, plus determination, will make it surprisingly easy for you to become an ex-smoker and to "kick" the habit permanently. This does not mean that you will never have the desire for another cigarette. It does mean that you can whip such desires readily.

If you undertake this program doubtfully, with your fingers crossed and on the basis, "Well, I'll try," then you may be able to stop, but it will be much more difficult to succeed. Your program is largely intended to develop the strong desire to stop smoking and to influence your subconscious mind through self-hypnosis so that it helps you stop by easing the desires to smoke.

Learning to hypnotize yourself will undoubtedly be an interesting experience for you. It can be valuable to you in other ways than in stopping smoking, and you will find it a definite asset to have this ability. It will help you to be more relaxed and freer of nervous tension and fatigue.

As a final word, it has now been some weeks since I smoked. I feel much better, I'm told my skin is clearer and my complexion is better. It's a relief not to be bothered with all the annoyances of smoking, such as dirty ashtrays, bad odors, etc. I hope you'll join me as an ex-smoker and I'm sure you'll have a similar experience.

MELVIN POWERS SELF-IMPROVEMENT